TOP HANDLE **MUST** COVER BOTTOM
HANDLE BEFORE YOU·START TO COOK

← CLOSE OPEN →

Prestige

Supercook's
COOKING UNDER PRESSURE

Marshall Cavendish

Pictures supplied by:
Bulloz 8L; Patrick Cocklin 82; Alan Duns
17, 18, 22, 25, 33, 46, 56, 84; Denis
Hughes-Gilbey 62; Paul Kemp 4, 12-3,
23, 34, 65, 66, 71, 75; Don Last 57, 58;
Max Logan 83; David Leldrum 44, 45T;
Roger Phillips 1, 2-3, 6, 9, 10, 14, 19, 26,
28, 30-1, 36, 37, 39, 40, 43, 45B, 51, 55,
59, 61, 67, 68, 73, 77, 78, 80, 85, 86-7, 88;
Iain Reid 20, 38; Red Saunders 48; Tower
Housewares Ltd 8R; John Turner 52.

Text prepared and edited by Linda Doeser
Published by Marshall Cavendish
Books Limited
58 Old Compton Street
London W1V 5PA

First printed 1977
Second printing 1981
Third printing 1982

Printed and bound by L.E.G.O., Vicenza, Italy

ISBN 0 85685 209 0

FOREWORD

Pressure cooking is making a come-back in a big way. These days its advantages are being appreciated by more and more budget-conscious cooks and the old myths about pressure cookers are being thrown out of the window. Safe, smart and easy to clean, modern pressure cookers save time, money and fuel, the food cooked in them is hygienically prepared, and it is more nourishing and tasty as well!

Anyone who owns a pressure cooker will know how vegetables can be cooked in a few minutes, how inexpensive cuts of meat become deliciously tender, how classic desserts like rice pudding take a fraction of their normal cooking time, even how simple and safe it is to use a pressure cooker for sterilizing baby equipment and food. But many people want to extend the use of their cookers to include more adventurous dishes, and it is often difficult to adapt recipes from ordinary cookbooks for use with a pressure cooker. *Cooking Under Pressure* has been planned to fill this gap. It contains a wide selection of recipes from many different countries for soups, vegetables, meat and fish, poultry and game, desserts and preserves. Using both ordinary and unusual ingredients, the recipes have all been tested so that accurate cooking times are given, no matter what type of cooker is used. The recipes can be used for a variety of occasions from a quick, informal lunch to a smart dinner party. Arranged in sections for easy reference, there are hints and tips too which will be useful both to experienced cooker owners and to those for whom pressure cooking is still a novelty.

A pressure cooker is probably one of the best investments for any kitchen. *Cooking Under Pressure* will help you make the most of it.

CONTENTS

INTRODUCTION

All food that is cooked is prepared by heating in a variety of ways—in an oven, in a saucepan of water, in a frying-pan, in steam. Pressure cooking is rather like an elaborate combination of saucepan and steamer. When a saucepan of water boils, at sea level, the water and the steam from it reach a temperature of 100°C (212°F). No matter how long you continue to boil, the temperature will never increase; the water will simply vapourize as steam and drift away until the saucepan boils dry.

A pressure cooker is designed to trap the steam and so increase the pressure, safely and easily. The principle involved is simply, the higher the pressure, the higher the temperature of boiling water.

Pressure at sea level	100°C	212°F
LOW pressure	109°C	228°F
MEDIUM pressure	115°C	240°F
HIGH pressure	121°C	250°F

Food in a pressure cooker is cooked by super-heated steam which forces its way through the food tenderizing it and cutting down cooking times by as much as 70 per cent.

These high temperatures mean that tough protein fibres are tenderized quickly, starch grains soften and generally all types of food retain their texture, colour and flavour. Soluble proteins and vital mineral salts are preserved and the short cooking time minimizes the loss of vitamins.

Different foods require different pressure and most kinds of cookers have three different pressures, LOW, MEDIUM and HIGH, sometimes called 5lb, 10lb and 15lb.

LOW pressure (5lb) is used for steaming puddings that contain a raising agent and for bottling fruit.

MEDIUM pressure (10lb) is used for softening fruit for jam, marmalade, etc. and vegetable bottling.

Opposite : Delicious, traditional steak and kidney pudding can be made in an hour with a pressure cooker (see page 45).
Below : The parts of an average cooker. Most parts are replaceable and reputable brands of cooker usually have a manufacturer's guarantee for at least five years.

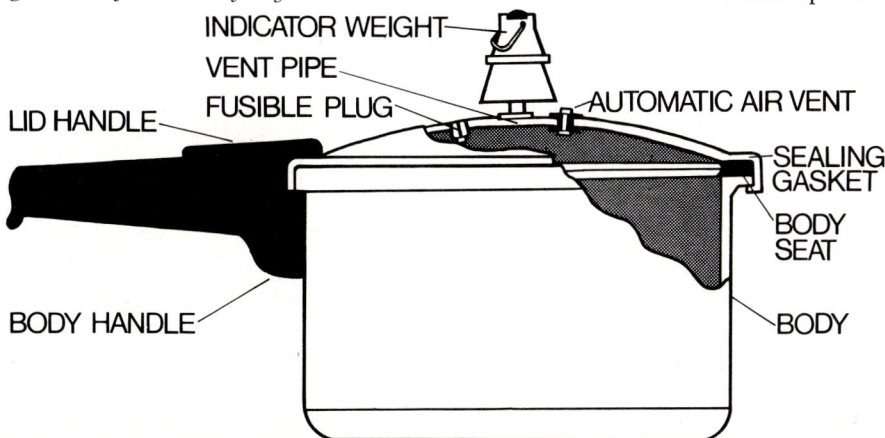

HIGH pressure (15lb) is the most commonly used for ordinary cooking.

Some cookers have a fixed pressure of 15lb, HIGH. They can be used for almost all kinds of cooking but are not really suitable for fruit bottling. They can be used quite successfully for steamed puddings, which are normally cooked at LOW (5lb) pressure but the puddings should be put in individual-sized basins and not one big one.

There are many different manufacturers of pressure cookers and choosing between them is a matter of personal taste, price etc. However, there are basically two types—the 'casserole and the 'saucepan'. The former has a small handle either side and often has only fixed, HIGH (15lb) pressure. The latter has two long handles and looks like a giant saucepan. Again, selection is a matter of personal taste, available storage space etc.

It is advisable to buy the largest cooker you can afford and find storage space for. Small meals can always be cooked in a large cooker but a small cooker is more limited.

Pressure cookers can be used on any sort of heat—gas, electricity, oil or solid fuel and are ideal for single people in bed sitting rooms or for students.

The cooker consists basically of three parts—the body, the cover and the indicator weight. The cover fits tightly on to the body forming a seal. When in use, the handles should be in alignment.

There are three main types of indicator weight. The fixed pressure weight is usually a lever type fitted with a spring valve. A second type has a sliding centre which rises at three stages, LOW (5lb), MEDIUM (10lb) and HIGH (15lb). The third type has three sections; inner weight for LOW (5lb), a screw-on sleeve MEDIUM (10lb) and an outer sleeve, HIGH (15lb).

All pressure cookers are supplied with a trivet—a stand on which to cook steamed puddings and pot roasts. Most of them are also supplied with separators both perforated and unperforated for cooking vegetables and rice.

All pressure cookers are fitted with a fusible safety device of some sort which allows steam to escape if excess pressure builds up. This is a legal requirement.

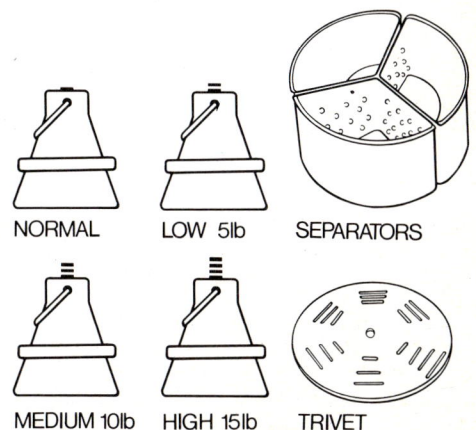

INDICATOR WEIGHT
VENT PIPE
FUSIBLE PLUG
LID HANDLE
AUTOMATIC AIR VENT
SEALING GASKET
BODY SEAT
BODY HANDLE
BODY

NORMAL   LOW 5lb   SEPARATORS

MEDIUM 10lb   HIGH 15lb   TRIVET

INTRODUCTION

All parts of the pressure cooker, except the indicator weight should be washed in warm soapy water, rinsed and dried thoroughly. The indicator weight could corrode if immersed in water. Store the cooker in a dry place with the lid upside down to allow air to circulate so that the cooker does not become musty. Check the vents each time the cooker is used to ensure that they are not blocked.

The liquid used in a pressure cooker must be one that produces steam. Oil or fat alone are insufficient.

The liquid and the food are put in the cooker. The food may be placed on the trivet or casseroled directly in the liquid.

Close the lid, checking the handles are in alignment and the seal is firm. Fit the indicator weight and turn on the heat. The liquid boils and fills the cooker with steam. This drives air out through the vent which then seals automatically.

When the required pressure is reached, reduce the heat to low so that the pressure is just maintained. Begin timing at this point.

The amount of liquid depends on the cooking time. There should always be a minimum of 300ml (10 fl oz). The liquid can be stock, water, wine, soup, milk, cream, cider or any other suitable liquid which produces steam. It is often better to stir beer or cider for a short while before using it in a pressure cooker to dispose of some of the bubbles.

When cooking solid foods, do not fill the cooker more than two-thirds full to allow plenty of room for the steam to circulate. When cooking soup, pasta, cereals, or anything inclined to froth up, do not fill the cooker more than half full. If you are steaming, a little vinegar or lemon juice added to the water will prevent discolouration from hard water.

At the end of cooking, pressure can be reduced in two ways,

Above left: The first pressure cookers were amazing contraptions.
Above: Today's cookers are safe, smart, up-to-date and easy to clean.

either by allowing the cooker to cool at room temperature or by plunging it into cold water. Water should never be run over the cooker as the automatic vent could release and suck water in and so spoil the recipe.

The first method is always used for the following:

egg custards where a sudden drop in temperature would cause the pudding to curdle

milk puddings where a sudden drop in temperature would cause the milk to separate

steamed puddings containing a raising agent where a sudden drop in temperature would cause the pudding to sink

cereals, stews, soups and dried vegetables where a sudden drop in temperature would cause the contents to froth up and spurt out of the vent pipe, scalding anyone within reach

fruit bottling where a sudden drop in temperature would cause the jars to crack.

Always check the instructions given in the recipe.

Before attempting to remove the lid, check that the indicator weight is not registering any pressure and that the automatic vent is released. Remove the indicator weight. A large fork is a good way of doing this with some models. Then remove the lid. If it does not open easily this means that there is still pressure inside. Leave the cooker to cool further.

The recipes in this book have all been written especially for use with a pressure cooker and offer many tempting and exciting ideas. To adapt your own recipes, follow the guide given at the beginning of each chapter.

SOUPS

Nothing tastes quite so delicious or is quite so welcoming on a cold winter evening as home-made soup. But soup can take a long time to cook and involve such a lot of bother that, for many busy cooks, it is simply too much trouble. However, with a pressure cooker, nourishing and tasty soups for the family take no time at all and even special soups to make your dinner guests feel really welcome, can be prepared in half the time.

There was a time too, when no kitchen was without a supply of good fresh stock for making gravies and sauces or as a foundation for all sorts of soups. In these busy days, however, a jug of stock is a rare and delicious treat. With a pressure cooker, this excellent culinary tradition can be revived without any time-consuming bother.

General hints
Always break bones into small pieces in order to extract all the goodness.

Do not use starchy foods for making stock. Bread, milk, potatoes, green vegetables and thickened sauces and gravies are all unsuitable, as the resulting stock will not keep.

Also do not use water in which green vegetables have been cooked as this can ferment during cooking. Water in which other vegetables have been cooked is ideal, with the exception of that used for very strongly flavoured vegetables.

The trivet is not used when cooking soups. All the ingredients are placed together so that their flavours can intermingle freely. Do not fill the cooker more than half full. There must be plenty of room for the liquid to boil freely and for steam to form without the vent becoming blocked. Because evaporation is so slight, pressure cooked soups and stock are highly concentrated and can be diluted at the end of cooking to provide the required number of servings. Sometimes, especially with meaty soups and stock, it is best to bring the liquid to the boil in the open cooker before pressure cooking. This is because scum forms during the cooking. Remove this by skimming with a metal spoon.

Always allow the pressure to reduce at room temperature. Reducing the pressure rapidly with cold water could cause scalding hot soup to froth up and spurt out of the vent.

Fat should be carefully removed before serving. Lift off with a metal spoon when cold and solidified or skim off with a metal spoon when hot. Leave the layer of fat intact when storing stock in the refrigerator until you want to use it. Add thickening agents such as flour, cornflour [cornstarch], and beurre manié at the end of the main cooking time. If you are adding egg yolks or cream, heat the soup in the open cooker to warm it through but do not boil.

Be careful when cooking vegetables with a strong flavour. Too much of one type of vegetable can dominate the taste of the soup. Use rather less seasoning, particularly salt and pungent herbs like dill and sage, than you would in an ordinary saucepan. You will soon learn by experience what quantities produce exactly the right flavour for you.

Below : A simple broth is easy to make in a pressure cooker.

SOUPS

STOCK

about 1.75 litres (3 pints) [8 cups]
30-40 minutes HIGH pressure

Metric/Imperial

1kg (2lb) beef shin bone, cut into
   pieces
1 marrow bone, cut into pieces
2 litres (3½ pints) water
1 large onion, peeled and cut in half
2 carrots, scraped and cut into big
   pieces
1 large leek, washed and cut in half
1 celery stalk
8 peppercorns
4 cloves
bouquet garni, consisting of 4 parsley
   sprigs, 1 thyme spray, and 1 bay leaf
   tied together
2 teaspoons salt

American

2lb beef shin bones, cut into pieces
1 marrow bone, cut into pieces
9 cups water
1 large onion, peeled and cut in half
2 carrots, scraped and cut into big
   pieces
1 large leek, washed and cut in half
1 celery stalk
8 peppercorns
4 cloves
bouquet garni, consisting of 4 parsley
   sprigs, 1 thyme spray and 1 bay leaf
   tied together
2 teaspoons salt

Remove the trivet from the pressure
cooker. Place the bones in the cooker
and pour over the water. Bring to the
boil slowly over low heat in the open
cooker. Using a metal spoon, skim off
the scum as it rises to the surface.
Continue to remove the scum as it
rises.

When the scum stops rising, add the
remaining ingredients and bring to
HIGH pressure. Cook for 30 to 40
minutes.

Allow the pressure to reduce at room
temperature.

Pour the stock through a strainer,
lined with two layers of cheesecloth,
into a large bowl. If you are going to
use the stock immediately, allow it to
cool and then remove the fat. If you
are storing the stock, leave the layer
of fat intact.

FISH STOCK

about 2.5 litres (4 pints) [10 cups]
15 minutes HIGH pressure

Metric/Imperial

1.25kg (3lb) fish bones, heads and
   trimmings
bouquet garni, consisting of 4 parsley
   sprigs, 1 thyme spray and 1 bay leaf
   tied together
1 celery stalk, chopped
1 large onion, peeled and sliced
2 carrots, scraped and sliced
1 teaspoon salt
6 peppercorns
juice of ½ lemon
2 litres (4 pints) water
225ml (8fl oz) white wine

American

3lb fish bones, heads and trimmings
bouquet garni, consisting of 4 parsley
   sprigs, 1 thyme spray and 1 bay leaf
   tied together
1 celery stalk, chopped
1 large onion, peeled and sliced
2 carrots, scraped and sliced
1 teaspoon salt
6 peppercorns
juice of ½ lemon
10 cups water
1 cup white wine

Thoroughly wash the fish pieces in cold
water.

Remove the trivet from the cooker.
Put all the ingredients in the cooker.
Bring to the boil in the open cooker.
Using a metal spoon, skim off any scum
that rises to the surface.

Bring to HIGH pressure and cook
for 15 minutes.

Allow the pressure to reduce at room
temperature.

Strain the stock into a large bowl.
Discard the contents of the strainer.
Use immediately or store in the
refrigerator.

FABADA

6 servings
20 minutes HIGH pressure
5 minutes HIGH pressure

Metric/Imperial

1.75 litres (3 pints) water

225g (8oz) dried haricot beans, soaked
   for 1 hour in hot water and drained
1 large onion, peeled and chopped
2 garlic cloves, crushed
4 bacon slices, chopped
2 morcillas or 125g (4oz) similar
   blood sausage, sliced
1 teaspoon dried oregano
2 small chorizo sausages, sliced
50g (2oz) smoked ham, chopped
¼ teaspoon ground saffron
½ teaspoon salt
½ teaspoon black pepper
½ teaspoon tabasco sauce

American

7½ cups water
1 cup (½lb) dried haricot beans, soaked
   for 1 hour in hot water and drained
1 large onion, peeled and chopped
2 garlic cloves, crushed
4 bacon slices, chopped
2 morcillas or ¼lb similar blood
   sausage, sliced
1 teaspoon dried oregano
2 small chorizo sausages, sliced
2oz smoked ham, chopped
¼ teaspoon ground saffron
½ teaspoon salt
½ teaspoon black pepper
½ teaspoon tabasco sauce

Remove the trivet. Pour the water into
the pressure cooker and add the beans,
onion and garlic. Bring to HIGH
pressure and cook for 20 minutes.

Allow the pressure to reduce at room
temperature.

In a small frying-pan, fry the bacon
over low heat for 5 minutes or until it
has rendered most of its fat. With a
slotted spoon, remove the bacon pieces
and drain on kitchen paper towels.

Add the bacon, morcillas or blood
sausage, oregano, chorizo sausages,
ham, saffron, salt, pepper and tabasco
to the cooker and stir to mix. Bring to
HIGH pressure and cook for 5 minutes.

Allow the pressure to reduce at room
temperature.

Pour the soup into a warmed tureen
and serve immediately.

*Fabada or Spanish Bean and Sausage
Soup is a filling meal in itself. Dried beans
usually take a couple of hours to cook
properly, but in a pressure cooker this
soup takes a total of half an hour,
excluding preparation time.*

SOUPS

PEA SOUP WITH HAM

4-6 servings
40 minutes High pressure
15 minutes HIGH pressure

Metric/Imperial

1 ham hock, soaked overnight and
    drained
1.5 litres (2½ pints) water
bouquet garni, consisting of 4 parsley
    sprigs, 1 thyme spray and 1 bay leaf
    tied together
1 teaspoon salt
1 teaspoon black pepper
25g (1oz) butter
1 medium-sized onion, peeled and
    sliced
1 garlic clove, crushed
2 small carrots, scraped and sliced
225g (8oz) split peas, soaked for 1 hour
    in hot water and drained

American

1 ham hock, soaked overnight and
    drained
5½ cups water
bouquet garni, consisting of 4 parsley
    sprigs, 1 thyme spray and 1 bay leaf
    tied together
1 teaspoon salt
1 teaspoon black pepper
2 tablespoons butter
1 medium-sized onion, peeled and
    sliced
1 garlic clove, crushed
2 small carrots, scraped and sliced
1 cup (½lb) split peas, soaked for 1 hour
    in hot water and drained

Remove the trivet. Place the ham hock in the cooker and pour over 1.2 litres (2 pints) [5 cups] of the water. Add the bouquet garni, salt and the black pepper. Bring to the boil in the open cooker over moderate heat and skim off any scum that rises to the surface.

Bring to HIGH pressure and cook for 40 minutes.

Allow the pressure to reduce at room temperature.

Using two large spoons, transfer the ham hock to a plate. Cover it with aluminium foil and set aside to cool.

Strain the cooking liquid into a large mixing bowl and set aside to cool at room temperature. When it is cool, place the liquid in the refrigerator and chill for 2 hours or until a layer of fat

has formed on the top of the liquid. Remove and discard the layer of fat and set the cooking liquid aside.

In the open cooker, melt the butter over moderate heat. When the foam subsides, add the onion, garlic and carrots and fry, stirring occasionally, for 5 to 7 minutes or until the onion is soft and translucent but not brown.

Add the split peas to the cooker and cook, stirring constantly for 5 minutes.

Add the cooking liquid and the remaining water. Bring to HIGH pressure and cook for 15 minutes.

Allow the pressure to reduce at room temperature.

Purée the mixture in an electric blender or a food mill. Set aside.

Using a sharp knife, cut the meat from the reserved ham hock. Discard any fat. Chop the meat into small pieces and add it to the purée.

Return the soup to the open cooker and simmer for 10 minutes or until it is heated through.

Transfer the soup to a warmed tureen and serve immediately.

COCK-A-LEEKIE

8 servings
30 minutes HIGH pressure

Metric/Imperial

1 × 1.5kg (1 × 3lb) chicken
2.5 litres (4 pints) water
7 leeks, including 5cm (2in) of the
    green stems, thoroughly washed and
    cut into 1cm (½in) slices
2 celery stalks, chopped
50g (2oz) pearl barley
bouquet garni, consisting of 4 parsley
    sprigs, 1 thyme spray and 1 bay leaf
    tied together
12 peppercorns tied in a piece of muslin
2 teaspoons salt
1 tablespoon chopped parsley

American

1 x 3lb chicken
10 cups water
7 leeks, including 2in of the green
    stems, thoroughly washed and cut
    into ½in slices
2 celery stalks, chopped
¼ cup pearl barley
bouquet garni, consisting of 4 parsley
    sprigs, 1 thyme spray and 1 bay leaf

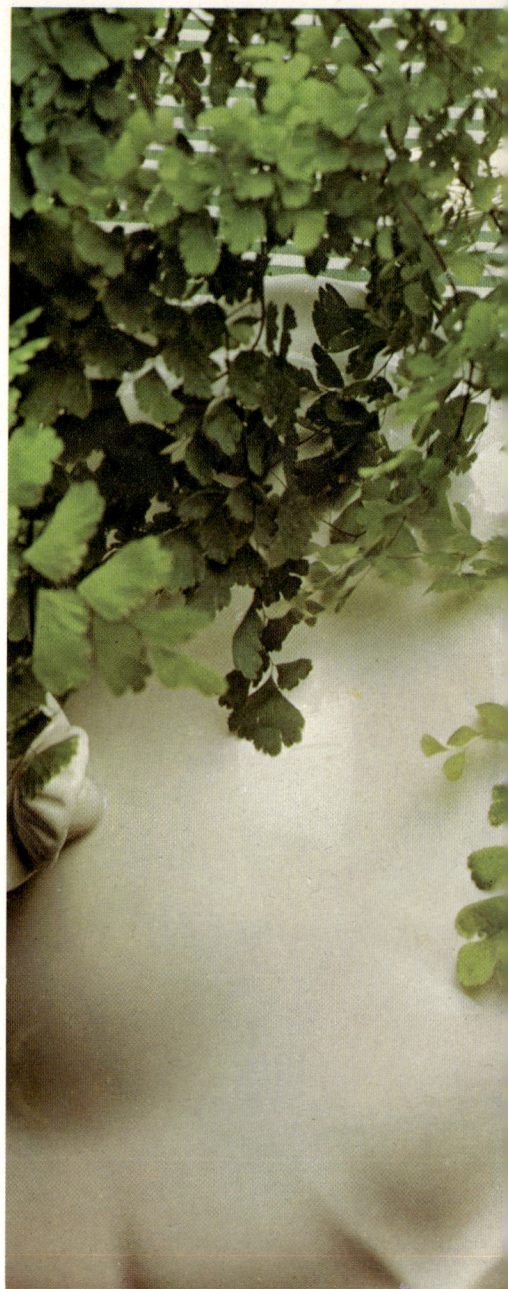

Tasty and nourishing, Pea Soup with Ham makes a wonderfully warming start to lunch or supper, and it is very economical as well, using generally very cheap ingredients.

    tied together
12 peppercorns tied in a piece of
    cheesecloth
2 teaspoons salt
1 tablespoon chopped parsley

Remove the trivet. Put the chicken in the pressure cooker and pour over the water. Bring the water to the boil in the open cooker. Using a metal spoon, remove any scum that rises to the surface.

Add the leeks, celery, barley, bouquet

garni, peppercorns and salt. Bring to HIGH pressure and cook for 30 minutes.

Allow the pressure to reduce at room temperature.

Transfer the chicken to a wooden board and leave until it is cool enough to handle. With a metal spoon, skim the fat off the surface of the cooking liquid. Remove and discard the bouquet garni and the peppercorns.

With a small, sharp knife, carefully detach the chicken meat from the skin and bones. Discard the skin and bones. Shred the meat and return it to the cooking liquid.

Simmer the soup for 5 minutes in the open cooker to reheat it thoroughly.

Remove the cooker from the heat and pour the soup into a warmed tureen. Sprinkle the parsley over the soup and serve immediately.

CREAM OF CARROT SOUP

4 servings
6 minutes HIGH pressure

Metric/Imperial

500g (1lb) carrots, scraped and sliced
1 litre (1½ pints) chicken stock
1 teaspoon salt
25g (1oz) butter
1 tablespoon flour
2 teaspoons tomato purée
125ml (4fl oz) single cream
¼ teaspoon white pepper
1 tablespoon chopped parsley

American

1 lb carrots, scraped and sliced
4 cups chicken stock
1 teaspoon salt
2 tablespoons butter
1 tablespoon flour
2 teaspoons tomato purée
½ cup light cream
¼ teaspoon white pepper
1 tablespoon chopped parsley

Remove the trivet. Put the carrots in the pressure cooker and pour over the chicken stock. Add half the salt. Bring to HIGH pressure and cook for 6 minutes.

Minestrone is probably one of the best-known Italian dishes. It is colourful and fresh-tasting, and cooked in a pressure cooker its nourishing ingredients retain all their goodness.

Allow the pressure to reduce at room temperature.

Pour the mixture through a strainer placed over a large bowl and reserve the liquid.

Purée the carrots in a food mill or a blender and set aside.

Melt the butter over moderate heat in the open cooker. Remove the cooker from the heat and gradually stir in the flour to make a smooth paste. Return the cooker to the heat and stir in about half the reserved stock and the carrot purée. Add the remaining stock and bring the mixture to the boil, stirring constantly.

Remove the cooker from the heat and stir in the tomato purée and the cream, mixing briskly, until all the ingredients are thoroughly blended.

Return the open cooker to low heat. Heat the soup gently until it is hot but not boiling. Add the remaining salt and the pepper.

Pour the soup into a warmed tureen. Sprinkle the parsley over the soup and serve immediately.

MINESTRONE

8 servings
20 minutes HIGH pressure
8 minutes HIGH pressure

Metric/Imperial

600ml (1 pint) water
125g (4oz) dried kidney beans, soaked for 1 hour in hot water and drained
50g (2oz) chick-peas, soaked for 1 hour in hot water and drained
175g (6oz) salt pork, cut into cubes
4 tablespoons olive oil
2 medium-sized onions, finely chopped
1 garlic clove, crushed
2 medium-sized potatoes, peeled and diced
4 carrots, scraped and cut into 2cm ($\frac{1}{2}$in) lengths
4 celery stalks, trimmed and cut into 2cm ($\frac{1}{2}$in) lengths
$\frac{1}{2}$ small cabbage, coarse outer leaves removed, washed and finely shredded
6 medium-sized tomatoes, blanched, peeled, seeded and coarsely chopped
2 tablespoons tomato purée
2 litres (3$\frac{1}{2}$ pints) hot chicken stock
bouquet garni, consisting of 4 parsley sprigs, 1 thyme spray and 1 bay leaf tied together
$\frac{1}{2}$ teaspoon salt
1 teaspoon black pepper
1 teaspoon dried oregano
225g (8oz) fresh peas, weighed after shelling
50g (2oz) macaroni
50g (2oz) Parmesan cheese, finely grated

American

2$\frac{1}{2}$ cups water
$\frac{2}{3}$ cup dried kidney beans, soaked for 1 hour in hot water and drained
$\frac{1}{3}$ cup chick-peas, soaked for 1 hour in hot water and drained
6oz salt pork, cut into cubes
4 tablespoons olive oil
2 medium-sized onions, finely chopped
1 garlic clove, crushed
2 medium-sized potatoes, peeled and diced
4 carrots, scraped and cut into $\frac{1}{2}$in lengths
4 celery stalks, trimmed and cut into $\frac{1}{2}$in lengths
$\frac{1}{2}$ small cabbage, coarse outer leaves removed, washed and finely shredded
6 medium-sized tomatoes, blanched, peeled, seeded and coarsely chopped
2 tablespoons tomato purée
2 quarts hot chicken stock

bouquet garni, consisting of 4 parsley
   sprigs, 1 thyme spray and 1 bay leaf
   tied together
½ teaspoon salt
1 teaspoon black pepper
1 teaspoon dried oregano
½lb fresh peas, weighed after shelling
½ cup macaroni
½ cup finely grated Parmesan cheese

Remove the trivet. Pour the water into the open cooker and bring to the boil over high heat. Add the beans and chick-peas. Bring to HIGH pressure and cook for 20 minutes.

Allow the pressure to reduce at room temperature.

Drain the beans and peas in a colander and set aside.

In the open cooker, fry the salt pork over moderate heat for 8 to 10 minutes, or until it is golden brown all over and has rendered most of its fat. Using a slotted spoon, transfer the salt pork to a plate and set aside.

Pour the olive oil into the pork fat and add the onions and garlic. Fry them, stirring occasionally, for 5 to 7 minutes, or until the onions are soft and translucent but not brown. Add the potatoes, carrots and celery to the cooker and continue to cook for a further 5 minutes, stirring constantly. Stir in the cabbage and cook for 5 minutes.

Add the tomatoes, tomato purée, hot chicken stock, bouquet garni, reserved beans and chick-peas, salt pork, salt, pepper, oregano, fresh peas and macaroni. Bring to HIGH pressure and cook for 8 minutes.

Allow the pressure to reduce at room temperature.

Remove and discard the bouquet garni. Pour the soup into a warmed tureen. Sprinkle over the Parmesan cheese and serve immediately.

CREAM OF TOMATO SOUP

4 servings
4 minutes HIGH pressure

Metric/Imperial

40g (1½oz) butter
1 shallot, finely chopped
700g (1½lb) ripe tomatoes, blanched,
   peeled, seeded and coarsely chopped
½ teaspoon sugar
bouquet garni, consisting of 4 parsley

sprigs, 1 thyme spray and 1 bay leaf
   tied together
½ teaspoon salt
½ teaspoon black pepper
¼ teaspoon dried basil
2 tablespoons tomato purée
1 litre (1¾ pints) hot chicken stock
1 tablespoon flour
125ml (4fl oz) single cream
1 tablespoon chopped chives

American

3 tablespoons butter
1 shallot, finely chopped
1½lb ripe tomatoes, blanched, peeled,
   seeded and coarsely chopped
½ teaspoon sugar
bouquet garni consisting of 4 parsley
   sprigs, 1 thyme spray and 1 bay leaf
   tied together
½ teaspoon salt
½ teaspoon black pepper
¼ teaspoon dried basil
2 tablespoons tomato puree
4 cups hot chicken stock
1 tablespoon flour
½ cup light cream
1 tablespoon chopped chives

Remove the trivet. Melt 1 tablespoon of the butter in the open cooker over low heat. When the foam subsides, add the shallot and cook for 5 minutes. Add the tomatoes, sugar, bouquet garni, salt, pepper, basil and tomato purée and cook for 5 minutes, stirring frequently. Stir in the stock. Bring to HIGH pressure and cook for 4 minutes.

Allow the pressure to reduce at room temperature.

Pour the mixture through a strainer placed over a large bowl. Reserve the liquid and discard the contents of the strainer.

Melt the remaining butter in the open cooker over moderate heat. Remove the pan from the heat and stir in the flour, mixing to a smooth paste. Return the cooker to the heat and mix in the reserved, strained tomato mixture. Bring the mixture to the boil.

Remove the cooker from the heat and stir in the cream, mixing briskly until all the ingredients are thoroughly blended. Reduce the heat to low and return the open cooker to the heat. Heat the soup very gently until it is hot but not boiling.

Pour the soup into a warmed tureen

and sprinkle over the chives. Serve immediately.

SCOTCH BROTH

4-6 servings
12 minutes HIGH pressure

Metric/Imperial

1.5kg (3lb) neck of mutton or lamb,
   chined and trimmed of excess fat
1.5 litres (2½ pints) water
2 teaspoons salt
1 teaspoon black pepper
50g (2oz) pearl barley
50g (2oz) green split peas
1 large carrot, scraped and chopped
1 large onion, peeled and chopped
2 leeks, trimmed, washed and chopped
2 celery stalks, trimmed and chopped
1 large turnip, peeled and coarsely
   chopped
2 tablespoons chopped fresh parsley

American

3lb neck of mutton or lamb, chined
   and trimmed of excess fat
5½ cups water
2 teaspoons salt
½ teaspoon black pepper
¼ cup pearl barley
¼ cup green split peas
1 large carrot, scraped and chopped
1 large onion, peeled and chopped
2 leeks, trimmed, washed and chopped
2 celery stalks, trimmed and chopped
1 large turnip, peeled and coarsely
   chopped
2 tablespoons chopped fresh parsley

Cut the meat into approximately 10cm (4in) pieces.

Remove the trivet from the pressure cooker. Put the meat into the cooker and pour over the water. Bring the liquid to the boil in the open cooker over moderately high heat. Skim off any scum that rises to the surface.

Add the salt, pepper, barley, peas, carrot, onion, leeks, celery and turnip. Bring to HIGH pressure and cook for 12 minutes.

Allow the pressure to reduce at room temperature.

Using kitchen tongs, transfer the meat to a chopping board. Using a sharp knife, slice the meat from the bones. Discard the bones.

Return the meat to the soup. Simmer the soup for 5 minutes in the open cooker to heat it through. Taste and add more seasoning if necessary.

Pour the soup into a warmed tureen. Sprinkle over the parsley and serve immediately.

LENTIL and VEGETABLE SOUP

6 servings
20 minutes HIGH pressure

Metric/Imperial

500g (1lb) lentils, soaked for 1 hour in hot water and drained
1.75 litres (3 pints) cold water
1 ham bone or knuckle (optional)
225g (8oz) lean bacon, in one piece
1 leek, trimmed, cleaned and chopped
2 large carrots, scraped and chopped
1 parsnip, peeled and chopped
2 celery stalks, chopped
1 teaspoon salt
2 tablespoons vegetable oil
2 medium-sized onions, peeled, and finely chopped
2 tablespoons flour
1½ tablespoons cider vinegar
225g (8oz) garlic sausage, diced
¼ teaspoon dried thyme
½ teaspoon black pepper

American

1lb lentils, soaked for 1 hour in hot water and drained
8 cups cold water
1 ham bone or knuckle (optional)
½lb lean bacon, in one piece
1 leek, trimmed, cleaned and chopped
2 large carrots, scraped and chopped
1 parsnip, peeled and chopped
2 celery stalks, chopped
1 teaspoon salt
2 tablespoons vegetable oil
2 medium-sized onions, peeled and finely chopped
2 tablespoons flour
1½ tablespoons cider vinegar
½lb garlic sausage, diced
¼ teaspoon dried thyme
½ teaspoon black pepper

Remove the trivet. Pour the water into the open cooker and bring to the boil over high heat. Remove the cooker from the heat and add the lentils, ham bone or knuckle, if you are using it, bacon,

leek, carrots, parsnip, celery and ½ teaspoon of the salt. Return the cooker to the heat and bring to HIGH pressure and cook for 20 minutes.

Allow the pressure to reduce at room temperature.

Meanwhile, in a heavy frying-pan, heat the oil over moderate heat. When the oil is hot, add the onions and cook, stirring occasionally, for 5 to 7 minutes or until they are soft and translucent but not brown. Sprinkle the flour over the onions, reduce the heat to low and cook, stirring constantly, for 3 to 4 minutes, or until the flour turns golden brown. Do not let the flour burn.

Remove the frying-pan from the heat and add about a cupful of the soup to the mixture, stirring well with a wooden spoon until the mixture is thick and creamy. Stir in the vinegar. Set aside.

Remove the ham bone or knuckle from the soup and discard it. Remove the bacon from the soup and cut it into small pieces.

Return the bacon pieces to the soup and add the sausage, thyme, remaining salt, the pepper and the onion mixture to the cooker. Simmer the soup in the open cooker, stirring occasionally, for 4 to 5 minutes, until the sausage is heated through.

Pour the soup into a warmed tureen and serve immediately.

MULLIGATAWNY SOUP

6 servings
20 minutes HIGH pressure

Metric/Imperial

1.75 litres (3 pints) water
1 teaspoon salt
1 × 1.5kg (1 × 3lb) chicken, cut into six pieces and giblets reserved (excluding the liver)
5cm (2in) piece fresh root ginger, peeled and bruised
4 bay leaves
2cm (1½in) slice creamed coconut
40g (1½oz) butter
2 medium-sized onions, finely chopped
2 garlic cloves, crushed
½ teaspoon hot chilli powder
1 tablespoon ground coriander
1 teaspoon ground cumin
½ teaspoon black pepper
4 tablespoons ground almonds

1½ tablespoons gram or chick-pea flour

American

7½ cups water
1 teaspoon salt
1 x 3lb chicken, cut into six pieces and giblets reserved (excluding the liver)
2in piece fresh root ginger, peeled and crushed
2 bay leaves
1½in slice creamed coconut
3 tablespoons butter
2 medium-sized onions, finely chopped
2 garlic cloves, crushed
½ teaspoon hot chili powder
1 tablespoon ground coriander
1 teaspoon ground cumin
½ teaspoon black pepper
4 tablespoons ground almonds
1½ tablespoons gram or chick-pea flour

Remove the trivet from the pressure cooker. Place the water, salt, chicken pieces, giblets, ginger and bay leaves in the cooker. Bring to HIGH pressure and cook for 20 minutes.

Allow the pressure to reduce at room temperature.

Using a slotted spoon, transfer the chicken pieces to a chopping board and set aside to cool.

Pour the stock through a strainer placed over a large bowl. Reserve the liquid and discard the contents of the strainer. Stir in the creamed coconut and, when it has dissolved, set the stock mixture aside.

When the chicken pieces are cool enough to handle, cut all the meat off the bones, using a small sharp knife. Dice the meat and discard the skin and bones. Set the diced meat aside.

Melt the butter in the open cooker over moderate heat. When the foam subsides, add the onions and fry, stirring occasionally, for 8 to 10 minutes or until they are golden-brown.

Add the garlic, chilli powder, coriander, cumin and pepper and fry, stirring frequently, for 5 minutes.

Stir in the ground almonds and the gram or chick-pea flour and cook, stirring constantly, for 1 minute. Gradually add the stock mixture, stirring constantly. When the soup comes to the

Right : Lentil and Vegetable Soup is a perfect 'winter warmer'!

boil, stir in the diced chicken. Cook for 5 minutes to heat the chicken through.

Pour the soup into a warmed tureen and serve immediately.

CHICKEN AND SPRING VEGETABLE SOUP

4 servings
35 minutes HIGH pressure

Metric/Imperial

SOUP

1.5 litres (2½ pints) cold water
2 medium-sized onions, peeled and quartered
6 carrots, scraped, 3 coarsely chopped and 3 cut into matchstick shapes
4 celery stalks with leaves, cut in halves
8 peppercorns
3 teaspoons salt
2 bay leaves
1 teaspoon dried tarragon
1 × 1.5kg (1 × 3lb) boiling chicken with the giblets, excluding the liver

DUMPLINGS

140g (4½oz) flour
1 teaspoon baking powder
½ teaspoon salt
½ egg lightly beaten
50ml (2fl oz) milk

American

SOUP

5½ cups cold water
2 medium-sized onions, peeled and quartered
6 carrots, scraped, 3 coarsely chopped and 3 cut into matchstick shapes
4 celery stalks, with leaves, cut in halves
8 peppercorns
3 teaspoons salt
2 bay leaves
1 teaspoon dried tarragon
1 x 3lb boiling chicken with the giblets, excluding the liver

DUMPLINGS

1 cup flour
1 teaspoon baking powder
½ teaspoon salt
½ egg, lightly beaten
¼ cup milk

Remove the trivet from the cooker. Pour the water into the open cooker and bring to the boil over high heat. Add the onions, the coarsely chopped carrots, celery, peppercorns, salt, bay leaves, tarragon, chicken and giblets. Bring to HIGH pressure and cook for 35 minutes.

Allow the pressure to reduce at room temperature.

Using a slotted spoon, transfer the chicken to a chopping board. Set aside until it is cool enough to handle.

Strain the soup into a large bowl and set aside to cool. Discard the contents of the strainer.

Using a sharp knife, remove the chicken meat from the bones. Discard the skin and bones. Cut the meat into cubes and set aside.

When the soup is cool, remove the solidified fat from the top with a metal spoon. Pour the soup into the open cooker and bring it to the boil over high heat. Add the carrot matchsticks to the soup and reduce the heat to moderately low. Simmer for 10 minutes or until the carrots are tender.

Meanwhile, prepare the dumplings. Sift 125g (4oz) of the flour, the baking powder and salt into a medium-sized mixing bowl. Mix together the beaten egg and the milk in a cup. Gradually stir the milk and egg mixture into the flour with a wooden spoon. Add only enough liquid to make a firm dough— it should not be too wet. Sift the remaining flour over the dough and, with your fingers, form small balls about the size of walnuts.

When the carrots are tender, increase the heat under the open cooker to high. When the soup is boiling rapidly, drop in the balls of dough. Cook the dumplings for 4 to 5 minutes, or until they are fluffy and have risen to the top of the soup. Be careful not to overcook the dumplings or they will be heavy.

Stir in the reserved chicken pieces and simmer the soup for 1 minute to warm them through.

Ladle the soup and the dumplings into a warmed tureen and serve immediately.

ONION SOUP

4 servings
10 minutes HIGH pressure

Metric/Imperial

1 tablespoon butter
2 tablespoons vegetable oil

Left : Easy to prepare, Chicken Soup with Dumplings is a satisfying meal in itself, using readily-available ingredients.

1 garlic clove, crushed
1 small potato, peeled and chopped
8 medium-sized onions, peeled
600ml (1 pint) milk
600ml (1 pint) water
$\frac{1}{2}$ teaspoon salt
$\frac{1}{2}$ teaspoon black pepper
$\frac{1}{4}$ teaspoon dried sage
$\frac{1}{4}$ teaspoon dried thyme
1 tablespoon cornflour dissolved in
    3 tablespoons water
125ml (4fl oz) single cream

American

---

1 tablespoon butter
2 tablespoons vegetable oil
1 garlic clove, crushed
1 small potato, peeled and chopped
8 medium-sized onions, peeled
$2\frac{1}{2}$ cups milk
$2\frac{1}{2}$ cups water
$\frac{1}{2}$ teaspoon salt
$\frac{1}{2}$ teaspoon black pepper
$\frac{1}{4}$ teaspoon dried sage

$\frac{1}{4}$ teaspoon dried thyme
1 tablespoon cornstarch dissolved in
    3 tablespoons water
$\frac{1}{2}$ cup light cream

In a medium-sized frying-pan, melt the butter with the oil over low heat. When the foam subsides, add the garlic and cook, stirring occasionally, for 2 minutes. Increase the heat to moderately high. Add the potato and cook, stirring frequently, for 4 minutes or until it is brown.

Meanwhile, slice two of the onions and push the slices out into rings.

Using a slotted spoon, remove the potato from the pan and drain it on kitchen paper towels.

Add the onion rings to the frying-pan and cook them, stirring occasionally, for 5 to 7 minutes or until they are soft and translucent, but not brown. Remove the pan from the heat. Using a slotted spoon, remove the onion rings from the pan and place them to drain on kitchen paper towels. Set aside.

Place the remaining onions on a chopping board and chop them finely.

Remove the trivet from the pressure

cooker. Pour in the milk and water. Add the salt, pepper, sage, thyme, potato and raw, chopped onions. Bring to HIGH pressure and cook for 10 minutes.

Allow the pressure to reduce at room temperature.

Strain the onion mixture into a large bowl, pressing down the vegetables in the strainer with a wooden spoon to extract all the juices. Discard the contents of the strainer.

Return the strained soup to the cooker. Add the reserved onion rings and stir in the cornflour [cornstarch] mixture. Place the open cooker over moderate heat and, stirring constantly, bring the soup to the boil. Simmer for 1 minute, stirring constantly.

Remove the cooker from the heat. Stir in the cream and pour the soup into a warmed tureen. Serve immediately.

Below : This delicate Onion Soup is hard to beat for delicious taste, and ease and speed of preparation, especially if you use a pressure cooker. Serve it with croutons and chopped spring [green] onions for an interesting textural contrast.

VEGETABLES

Vegetables, generally, cook so rapidly in an ordinary saucepan that, at first sight, it doesn't seem worth using a pressure cooker. But this is not so, for a pressure cooker not only lessens the cooking time but, even more important, preserves the taste, texture and food value of vegetables.

Vegetables are rich in vitamins but these are often destroyed during cooking. However, in a pressure cooker the absence of air conserves them. Cooking in steam, rather than water also means that valuable mineral salts and proteins are not lost. Besides this valuable retention of nutritional content, cooking in steam also preserves the colour, texture and flavour of vegetables which makes them seem as if they were freshly picked from your own garden. If you are lucky enough to be able to grow your own vegetables, pressure cooking them will reward your hard work.

General hints for fresh vegetables

The freshness, age and the size of the pieces you cut vegetables into will affect the cooking time.

The following charts and recipes are intended as a general guide. However, as with other food-types you will soon learn through experience to adjust the cooking time for vegetables exactly the way you like them.

Do not prepare vegetables well in advance of cooking as they can dry out, lose their taste and be generally disappointing.

Wash them thoroughly in cold water and discard coarse outer leaves, thick stem, etc.

A minimum of 300ml (10fl oz) [1¼ cups] of water is necessary for cooking vegetables.

Both the trivet and the separators can be used. The essence of pressure cooking vegetables is that they do not cook in the water but in the steam. Consequently, if you are cooking several different vegetables, they still retain their separate flavours. Large vegetables, such as potatoes, can be cooked on the trivet and smaller ones, such as peas, can be cooked in the separators.

As each layer of vegetables is packed on to the trivet or into the separators, sprinkle it with salt and any herbs you wish to use. Pepper is best added afterwards.

If you are cooking a mixture of different size vegetables, or root and green vegetables together, cut them up so that they require the same amount of time.

When using the trivet for cooking vegetables, the cooker should not be more than two-thirds full to allow sufficient room for the steam to circulate.

Vegetables are cooked at HIGH pressure. Unless a specific recipe says otherwise, reduce the pressure with cold water as delay can result in overcooking.

The vegetables will not need to be drained. Use the concentrated liquid for sauces and gravies.

Fresh vegetables – cooking times (HIGH pressure)

Artichokes, globe	6-10 minutes
Artichokes, Jerusalem	4- 5 minutes
Asparagus	3- 4 minutes
Asparagus tips	1- 2 minutes
Aubergines [Eggplant]	1- 2 minutes
Beans, broad [lima]	3- 4 minutes
Beans, French [green]	3- 4 minutes
Beetroot [Beet], small	10 minutes
medium	20 minutes
large	30 minutes
Broccoli	3- 4 minutes
Brussels sprouts	3- 4 minutes
Cabbage (shredded)	3 minutes
Cabbage, red	4- 5 minutes
Carrots, young, whole	4 minutes
sliced	3- 4 minutes
quartered	4 minutes
Cauliflower, florets	3- 4 minutes
whole	6- 8 minutes
Celeriac	3 minutes
Celery	3 minutes
Chicory [Endive]	4- 6 minutes
Courgettes [Zucchini]	3- 4 minutes
Leeks	4 minutes
Marrow	4 minutes
Onions, sliced	4 minutes
whole	8-10 minutes
Parsnips, sliced	3- 4 minutes
quartered	6- 8 minutes
Peas	3- 4 minutes
Potatoes, new, whole	4- 6 minutes
old, halved	4- 6 minutes
old, quartered	3- 4 minutes
Spinach	bring to pressure only
Swedes [Rutabaga]	4 minutes
Sweetcorn (on the cob)	3- 5 minutes
Turnip	4 minutes

General hints for dried vegetables

An enormous amount of time and bother can be saved by pressure cooking dried vegetables. They no longer need be soaked overnight and then cooked for hours, although some soaking is necessary.

Wash the vegetables thoroughly. Put them in a basin and pour over enough boiling water to cover them. Place a plate on top and leave them for 1 hour.

Remove the trivet from the cooker and pour in 1 litre (1¾ pints) [1 quart] of water for every 500g (1lb) of dried vegetables. Bring to the boil in the open cooker before adding vegetables.

Add the vegetables and bring the liquid back to the boil. Skim off any scum that rises to the surface, using a metal spoon.

Reduce the heat so that the water is simmering and bring to HIGH pressure without adjusting it. Allow the pressure to reduce at room temperature.

Dried vegetables – cooking times (HIGH pressure)	
Butter beans	30 minutes
Haricot beans, large	25 minutes
small	20 minutes
Lentils	15 minutes
Peas, split	15 minutes
whole	20 minutes

Cooking times (HIGH pressure) giving water requirement		
Barley,		
pearl	2 litres (4 pints) per 225g (8oz)	20 minutes
Macaroni	1 litre (2 pints) per 225g (8oz)	4- 6 minutes
Noodles,		
alphabet	1 litre (2 pints) per 225g (8oz)	3- 4 minutes
fine	1 litre (2 pints) per 225g (8oz)	2- 3 minutes
medium	1 litre (2 pints) per 225g (8oz)	3- 4 minutes
shells	1.25 litres (2½ pints) per 225g (8oz)	3 minutes
Rice,		
long grain	700ml (1¼ pints) per 225g (8oz)	5 minutes
Oatmeal,		
coarse	1.25 litres (2½ pints) per 225g (8oz)	15-20 minutes
Spaghetti	1 litre (2 pints) per 225g (8oz)	5- 6 minutes
Vermicelli	1 litre (2 pints) per 225g (8oz)	3- 4 minutes

PASTA & CEREALS

These provide necessary carbohydrates and can make a welcome change in the family menu. The trivet is not used as they all require plenty of liquid to absorb during cooking.

Bring sufficient salted water to the boil in the open cooker. Plunge in the cereal, etc. Curl spaghetti into the cooker as it softens. Do not fill the cooker more than half full. Close the cooker and then fit the indicator weight. Bring to HIGH pressure and cook for the required time.

Allow the pressure to reduce at room temperature. Rice can be cooked in the unperforated separator if you wish to cook other foods.

Below : Pasta comes in a bewildering number of varieties, each with its own classic recipes and accompaniments. Here, (among others) can be seen various types of shell pasta, egg noodles, lasagna leaves and ravioli.

BRAISED CELERY AND BACON

4-6 servings
3 minutes HIGH pressure

Metric/Imperial

2 medium-sized heads of celery, cleaned and cut into 10cm (4in) pieces
175g (6oz) small onions, peeled and left whole
300ml (½ pint) water
bouquet garni, consisting of 4 parsley sprigs, 1 thyme spray and 1 bay leaf tied together
1 teaspoon salt
½ teaspoon black pepper
225g (8oz) streaky bacon, coarsely chopped
1 tablespoon butter

American

2 medium-sized heads of celery, cleaned and cut into 4in pieces
6oz small onions, peeled and left whole
1¼ cups water
bouquet garni, consisting of 4 parsley sprigs, 1 thyme spray and 1 bay leaf tied together
1 teaspoon salt
½ teaspoon black pepper
½lb bacon, coarsely chopped
1 tablespoon butter

Remove the trivet. Put the celery and onions in the cooker. Pour over the water and add the bouquet garni, salt and pepper. Bring to HIGH pressure and cook for 3 minutes.

Reduce the pressure with cold water.

Using a slotted spoon, transfer the celery and onions to a dish and set aside. Discard the cooking liquid.

In a large frying-pan, fry the bacon pieces over moderate heat. Add a little of the butter if extra fat is needed. When the bacon is crisp, add the remaining butter to the pan and allow it to melt. Add the celery and onions and cook the mixture over moderate heat for 10 minutes, or until the vegetables become lightly browned. Add more salt and pepper, if necessary. Transfer the mixture to a warmed serving dish and serve immediately.

Below : Peperonata is a colourful Italian vegetable stew. It is made with peppers, tomatoes and garlic and can be eaten hot or cold, with meat or on its own as a light vegetarian meal.

PEPERONATA

4-6 servings
3 minutes HIGH pressure

Metric/Imperial

25g (1oz) butter
2 tablespoons olive oil
1 large onion, peeled and thinly sliced
1 garlic clove, crushed
500g (1lb) red peppers, white pith removed, seeded and cut into strips
500g (1lb) tomatoes, blanched, peeled and chopped
½ teaspoon salt
¼ teaspoon black pepper
1 bay leaf
225ml (8fl oz) tomato juice

American

2 tablespoons butter
2 tablespoons olive oil
1 large onion, peeled and thinly sliced
1 garlic clove, crushed
1lb red peppers, white membranes removed, seeded and cut into strips
1lb tomatoes, blanched, peeled and chopped
½ teaspoon salt
¼ teaspoon black pepper

1 bay leaf
1 cup tomato juice

Remove the trivet. Melt the butter with the oil over moderate heat. When the foam subsides, add the onion and garlic and fry, stirring occasionally, for 5 to 7 minutes or until the onion is soft and translucent but not brown.

Add the red peppers, tomatoes, salt, pepper, bay leaf and tomato juice. Bring to HIGH pressure and cook for 3 minutes.

Allow the pressure to reduce at room temperature.

Remove and discard the bay leaf. Transfer the vegetables to a warmed serving dish and serve immediately, if you are serving the peperonata hot.

FENNEL, GREEK-STYLE

4 servings
3 minutes HIGH pressure

Metric/Imperial

2 heads of fennel
4 tablespoons olive oil
225g (8oz) small white onions, peeled and left whole
1 teaspoon salt
½ teaspoon white pepper
½ teaspoon cayenne pepper
½ teaspoon ground coriander
¼ teaspoon dried thyme
1 bay leaf
2 tablespoons tomato purée
50g (2oz) sultanas or raisins
150ml (5fl oz) warmed dry white wine

American

2 heads of fennel
4 tablespoons olive oil
8oz small white onions, peeled and left whole
1 teaspoon salt
½ teaspoon white pepper
½ teaspoon cayenne pepper
½ teaspoon ground coriander
¼ teaspoon dried thyme
1 bay leaf
2 tablespoons tomato purée
⅓ cup golden raisins or raisins
⅔ cup warmed dry white wine

Wash and trim the fennel and discard any withered outer leaves. Cut the heads into quarters and set aside.

Remove the trivet. Heat the oil in the open cooker over moderate heat. When the oil is hot, add the fennel pieces and small onions. Fry them, stirring occasionally for 4 to 5 minutes. Add the salt, pepper, cayenne, coriander, thyme, bay leaf, tomato purée and the sultanas [golden raisins] or raisins. Mix well to blend. Add the wine and bring to HIGH pressure. Cook for 3 minutes.

Reduce the pressure with cold water.

Transfer the vegetables to a warmed serving dish and serve immediately.

RATATOUILLE

4-6 servings as a first course
6-8 servings as accompanying vegetable
5 minutes HIGH pressure

Metric/Imperial

25g (1oz) butter
50ml (2fl oz) olive oil
2 large onions, peeled and sliced
2 garlic cloves, crushed
3 medium-sized aubergines, thinly sliced and lightly salted
1 large green pepper, white pith removed, seeded and chopped
1 large red pepper, white pith removed, seeded and chopped
5 medium-sized courgettes, trimmed and sliced
400g (14oz) canned, peeled tomatoes
150ml (5fl oz) water
1 teaspoon dried basil
1 teaspoon dried rosemary
1 teaspoon salt
¾ teaspoon black pepper
2 tablespoons chopped fresh parsley

American

2 tablespoons butter
4 tablespoons olive oil
2 large onions, peeled and sliced
2 garlic cloves, crushed
3 medium-sized eggplants, thinly sliced and lightly salted
1 large green pepper, white membrane removed, seeded and chopped
1 large red pepper, white membrane removed, seeded and chopped
5 medium-sized zucchinis, trimmed and sliced
14oz can peeled tomatoes
2/3 cup water
1 teaspoon dried basil
1 teaspoon dried rosemary
1 teaspoon salt
¾ teaspoon black pepper
2 tablespoons chopped fresh parsley

Remove the trivet. Melt the butter with the oil over moderate heat in the open cooker. When the foam subsides, add the onions and the garlic and fry, stirring occasionally, for 5 to 7 minutes, or until the onions are soft and translucent but not brown.

Add the aubergine [eggplant] slices, green and red peppers and courgette [zucchini] slices to the cooker. Fry for 5 minutes, shaking the cooker frequently. Add the tomatoes with their can juice and the water. Sprinkle over the basil, rosemary, salt, pepper and parsley. Bring to HIGH pressure and cook for 5 minutes.

Reduce the pressure with cold water.

If you are serving it cold, set aside to cool at room temperature. When cold, transfer to a serving dish and serve.

If you are serving it hot, transfer the vegetables to a warmed serving dish and serve immediately.

Ratatouille can be served in small portions as an accompanying vegetable or larger ones, as a first course.

CHANNA DHAL

6 servings
20 minutes HIGH pressure
5 minutes HIGH pressure

Metric/Imperial

350g (12oz) chick-peas, washed thoroughly, soaked in hot water for 1 hour and drained
1 litre (1¾ pints) water
1 teaspoon salt
3 tablespoons clarified or melted butter
½ teaspoon cumin seeds
1 medium-sized onion, peeled and finely chopped
3cm (1in) piece root ginger, peeled and finely chopped
½ teaspoon turmeric
¼ teaspoon ground cumin
½ teaspoon ground coriander
1 teaspoon garam masala
¼ teaspoon chilli powder
2 tablespoons water
1 tablespoon chopped coriander leaves

American

¾lb chick-peas, washed thoroughly, soaked in hot water for 1 hour and drained

4 cups water

1 teaspoon salt

3 tablespoon clarified or melted butter

½ teaspoon cumin seeds

1 medium-sized onion, peeled and finely chopped

1in piece of root ginger, peeled and finely chopped

½ teaspoon turmeric

¼ teaspoon ground cumin

½ teaspoon ground coriander

1 teaspoon garam masala

¼ teaspoon chili powder

2 tablespoons water

1 tablespoon chopped coriander leaves

Remove the trivet. Put the chick-peas in the cooker and pour over the water. Add the salt. Bring the liquid to the boil in the open cooker over moderate heat. Bring to HIGH pressure and cook for 20 minutes.

Allow the pressure to reduce at room temperature.

Transfer the peas and the liquid to a large bowl.

Heat the clarified or melted butter in the open cooker over low heat. Add the cumin seeds and cook for 1 minute. Add the onion and cook for 5 minutes, stirring frequently. Stir in the ginger and continue cooking for 4 minutes, or until the onion becomes golden brown.

In a small bowl, combine the turmeric, ground cumin, coriander, garam masala and chilli powder with the 2 tablespoons of water to make a paste.

Add the paste to the onion mixture and fry for 3 to 4 minutes, stirring constantly. Add the chick-peas and the cooking liquid, stirring constantly. Increase the heat to moderate and, stirring constantly, bring the mixture to the boil. Bring to HIGH pressure and cook for 5 minutes.

Reduce the pressure with cold water.

Taste the chick peas and add more salt if necessary. Pour the mixture into a warmed serving dish. Sprinkle the top with the chopped coriander leaves and serve immediately.

Channa Dhal is an inexpensive thick pea curry which could be served as a meal in itself with chapattis (hot Indian bread), raita (yogurt) and mango chutney, or as part of a selection of curry dishes at a dinner party.

STUFFED ONIONS

4-6 servings
3 minutes HIGH pressure
12 minutes HIGH pressure

Metric/Imperial

600ml (1 pint) water
6 large Spanish onions, peeled
1 teaspoon salt
125g (4oz) cooked chicken, minced
4 tablespoons canned sweetcorn,
  drained
1 small carrot, scraped and grated
2 tablespoons sultanas or raisins
50g (2oz) plus 2 tablespoons fresh
  brown breadcrumbs
¼ teaspoon black pepper
½ teaspoon dried sage
1 tablespoon chopped fresh parsley
1 egg, lightly beaten
25g (1oz) plus 1 teaspoon butter
125ml (4fl oz) dry white wine

American

2½ cups water
6 large Spanish onions, peeled
1 teaspoon salt
4oz cooked chicken, ground
4 tablespoons canned corn, drained
1 small carrot, scraped and grated
2 tablespoons golden raisins or raisins
1 cup plus 2 tablespoons fresh
  wholewheat breadcrumbs
¼ teaspoon black pepper
½ teaspoon dried sage
1 tablespoon chopped fresh parsley
1 egg, lightly beaten
2 tablespoons plus 1 teaspoon butter
½ cup dry white wine

Pour 300ml (½ pint) of the water into the cooker. Arrange the onions on the trivet and sprinkle over ½ teaspoon of the salt. Bring to HIGH pressure and cook for 3 minutes.

Allow the pressure to reduce at room temperature.

Discard the cooking liquid. Using a large spoon, transfer the onions to a chopping board. Using a sharp knife, cut across the tops of the onions, 2cm (¾in) from the top. Discard the tops. Cut a very thin slice from the bottom to give the onions a flat surface to rest on. Using a teaspoon, carefully scoop out the middle of each onion, leaving a 1cm (½in) shell. Set the onion shells aside. Discard one half of the scooped-out onion. Chop the remainder and place it in a large mixing bowl.

Above : Stuffed Onions may be served as a first course, as part of an hors d'oeuvre or as a light meal.

Add the chicken, sweetcorn, carrot, sultanas [golden raisins] or raisins, 50g (2oz) of the breadcrumbs, the remaining salt, ⅛ teaspoon of the pepper, the sage, parsley and egg to the onion in the mixing bowl. With a fork, combine all the ingredients thoroughly.

Spoon the stuffing into the onion shells, doming it up in the centre. Dot with 25g (1oz) of the butter, cut into small pieces. Sprinkle over the remaining breadcrumbs and the remaining pepper.

With the remaining butter, lightly grease a heatproof dish. Place the onions in the prepared dish and pour the wine around them. Cover with aluminium foil.

Pour the remaining water into the cooker. Place the dish on the trivet and bring to HIGH pressure. Cook for 12 minutes.

Allow the pressure to reduce at room temperature.

Remove the dish from the cooker and discard the aluminium foil. Serve immediately straight from the dish.

PETITS POIS A LA FRANCAISE

4-6 servings
4 minutes HIGH pressure

Metric/Imperial

300ml (½ pint) water
700g (1½lb) small, fresh, garden peas, weighed after shelling
1 teaspoon salt
½ teaspoon black pepper
1 teaspoon sugar
1 medium-sized onion, peeled and thinly sliced
4 lettuce leaves, washed, shaken dry and shredded
25g (1oz) beurre manié, made by blending 2 tablespoons butter with 4 tablespoons flour

American

1¼ cups water
1½lb small fresh garden peas, weighed after shelling
1 teaspoon salt
½ teaspoon black pepper
1 teaspoon sugar
1 medium-sized onion, peeled and thinly sliced
4 lettuce leaves, washed, shaken dry and shredded
2 tablespoons beurre manié, made by blending 2 tablespoons butter with 4 tablespoons flour

Remove the trivet and pour the water into the cooker. Add the peas, salt, pepper, sugar, onion and lettuce. Bring to HIGH pressure and cook for 4 minutes.

Reduce the pressure with cold water.

Return the open cooker to low heat and add the beurre manié, a little at a time, stirring constantly. Simmer the mixture for a further 2 minutes or until it has thickened.

Transfer the mixture to a warmed serving dish and serve immediately.

BRAISED RED CABBAGE

4-6 servings
5 minute HIGH pressure

Metric/Imperial

2 tablespoons butter
4 bacon slices, cut into thin strips
1 small carrot, scraped and sliced
2 medium-sized onions, peeled and sliced
1kg (2lb) red cabbage, washed and shredded
2 garlic cloves, crushed
1 bay leaf
¼ teaspoon ground cloves
¼ teaspoon grated nutmeg
½ teaspoon salt
¼ teaspoon black pepper
150ml (5fl oz) dry red wine
150ml (5fl oz) beef stock

American

2 tablespoons butter
4 bacon slices, cut into thin strips
1 small carrot, scraped and sliced
2 medium-sized onions, peeled and sliced
2lb red cabbage, washed and shredded
2 garlic cloves, crushed
1 bay leaf
¼ teaspoon ground cloves
¼ teaspoon grated nutmeg
½ teaspoon salt
¼ teaspoon black pepper
⅔ cup dry red wine
⅔ cup beef stock

Remove the trivet. Melt the butter in the open cooker over moderate heat. When the foam subsides, add the bacon, carrot and onions. Reduce the heat to low and cook, stirring occasionally, for 10 minutes.

Stir in the cabbage and continue to cook for a further 5 minutes. Add the garlic, bay leaf, cloves, nutmeg, salt, pepper, wine and stock. Bring to HIGH pressure and cook for 5 minutes.

Allow the pressure to reduce at room temperature.

Transfer the mixture to a warmed serving dish. Remove and discard the bay leaf and serve immediately.

BAKED BEANS, ITALIAN STYLE

4 servings
20 minutes HIGH pressure

Metric/Imperial

225g (8oz) dried white or red haricot beans, soaked in hot water for 1 hour and drained
3 garlic cloves, crushed
3 tablespoons chopped fresh basil or 1½ tablespoons dried basil
½ teaspoon salt
½ teaspoon black pepper
¼ teaspoon ground cinnamon
8 streaky bacon slices, coarsley chopped
600ml (1 pint) water

American

½lb dried white or red haricot beans, soaked in hot water for 1 hour and drained
3 garlic cloves, crushed
3 tablespoons chopped fresh basil or 1½ tablespoons dried basil
½ teaspoon salt
½ teaspoon black pepper
¼ teaspoon ground cinnamon
8 bacon slices, coarsely chopped
2½ cups water

Remove the trivet. Place the ingredients in the cooker. Stir to mix. Bring to HIGH pressure and cook for 20 minutes.

Allow the pressure to reduce at room temperature.

Strain off any excess liquid. Transfer the mixture to a warmed serving dish and serve immediately.

ERBSENPUREE

6 servings
15 minutes HIGH pressure

Metric/Imperial

725ml (1¼ pints) water
500g (1lb) yellow, split peas, soaked for 1 hour in hot water and drained
2 carrots, scraped and sliced
2 celery stalks, chopped
1 onion, peeled and cut in half
1 ham bone
¼ teaspoon dried thyme
½ teaspoon salt
25g (1oz) butter
1 large onion, sliced and pushed out into rings

American

3 cups water
2 cups (1lb) yellow split peas, soaked for 1 hour in hot water and drained
2 carrots, scraped and sliced
2 celery stalks, chopped
1 onion, cut in half

1 ham bone
$\frac{1}{4}$ teaspoon dried thyme
$\frac{1}{2}$ teaspoon salt
2 tablespoons butter
1 large onion, sliced and pushed out
    into rings

Remove the trivet. Pour the water into the cooker. Bring it to the boil, in the open cooker over moderately high heat. Add the peas, carrots, celery, onion halves, ham bone, thyme and salt. Bring to HIGH pressure and cook for 15 minutes.

Allow the pressure to reduce at room temperature.

Remove and discard the ham bone. Purée the vegetables in a food mill or an electric blender.

Transfer the purée to a warmed serving dish and keep hot while you prepare the onions.

In a small frying-pan, melt the butter over moderate heat. When the foam subsides, add the onion rings. Fry them, stirring occasionally, for 8 minutes, or until they are golden brown.

Scatter the onion rings on top of the purée to decorate it and serve the purée immediately.

MARROW WITH TOMATOES

4 servings
4 minutes HIGH pressure

Metric/Imperial

3 tablespoons vegetable oil
1 large onion, peeled and chopped
4 medium-sized tomatoes, blanched,
    peeled and sliced
125ml (4fl oz) tomato juice
1 teaspoon salt
1 teaspoon black pepper
1 teaspoon dried basil
$\frac{1}{4}$ teaspoon dried thyme
$\frac{1}{2}$ teaspoon dried marjoram
1kg (2lb) marrow, peeled, seeded and
    cut into small cubes
1 tablespoon chopped fresh chives
50g (2oz) Cheddar cheese grated
1 tablespoon grated Parmesan cheese

American

3 tablespoons vegetable oil
1 large onion, peeled and chopped
4 medium-sized tomatoes, blanched,
    peeled and sliced
$\frac{1}{2}$ cup tomato juice
1 teaspoon salt
1 teaspoon black pepper
1 teaspoon dried basil
$\frac{1}{4}$ teaspoon dried thyme
$\frac{1}{2}$ teaspoon dried marjoram
2lb zucchini, peeled and cut into cubes
1 tablespoon chopped fresh chives
$\frac{1}{2}$ cup grated Cheddar cheese
1 tablespoon grated Parmesan cheese

Remove the trivet. Heat the oil in the open cooker over moderate heat. Add the onion and cook, stirring occasionally, for 5 to 7 minutes or until it is soft and translucent but not brown.

Add the tomatoes and cook, stirring frequently, for 1 minute. Pour in the tomato juice and add the salt, pepper, basil, thyme and marjoram and cook, stirring occasionally, for 3 minutes. Add the marrow [zucchini]. Bring to HIGH pressure and cook for 4 minutes.

Allow the pressure to reduce at room temperature.

Sprinkle the chives and Cheddar cheese over the squash mixture and pour it into a warmed serving dish. Sprinkle over the Parmesan cheese and serve immediately.

Below : Marrow [Zucchini] with tomatoes.

FISH

The great advantage to pressure cooking fish is that it minimizes that all-pervading smell.

Fish contain a lot of protein as well as many other essential nutrients. Cooking in steam conserves these, either directly or in the cooking liquid which can be used for making a sauce. Pressure cooked fish tends to preserve its shape and texture rather better.

Pressure cooking is an ideal way to prepare fish for invalids, those on a special diet, or indeed, for slimmers.

Fish can be poached or steamed, using the trivet, or casseroled directly in the liquid. Some cooks prefer to wrap the fish in buttered, greaseproof or waxed paper or aluminium foil before steaming as this facilitates lifting it out in one piece.

For fish stock—see Soups recipes.

Frozen fish may be used and should be treated in the same way as fresh, except about half the liquid is needed. Do not thaw before cooking.

General hints

Clean and trim fins and tails, where necessary. Wash the fish and pat dry with kitchen paper towels. Rub half a teaspoon of salt and a half teaspoon of black pepper into each side.

The liquid can be water, wine, fish stock or cider. A minimum of 300ml (10fl oz) [1¼ cups] is required.

If you are poaching or steaming, grease the trivet lightly with 1 teaspoon of butter or wrap the fish in greaseproof or waxed paper, or aluminium foil, lightly greased with butter. Cook at HIGH pressure and at the end of cooking, reduce the pressure with cold water.

Cooking times (HIGH pressure)

Bream [Porgy]	steaks and fillets	4-6 minutes	**Plaice [Flounder]**	filleted	4-6 minutes
	tail and middle cut	5-6 minutes per 500g (1lb)		whole	5-8 minutes
Brill	steaks and fillets	4-6 minutes	**Prawns**		2-3 minutes
	tail and middle cut	5-6 minutes per 500g (1lb)	**Rock salmon**	steaks and fillets	4-6 minutes
Cod	steaks and fillets	4-6 minutes		tail and middle cut	5-6 minutes per 500g (1lb)
	tail and middle cut	5-6 minutes per 500g (1lb)	**Salmon**	steaks	4-6 minutes
Crab		7-10 minutes		tail and middle cut	6 minutes per 500g (1lb)
Haddock	steaks and fillets	4-6 minutes	**Salmon trout**	steaks	4-6 minutes
	tail and middle cut	5-6 minutes per 500g (1lb)		tail and middle cut	6 minutes per 500g (1lb)
Hake	steaks and fillets	4-6 minutes	**Shrimps**		2-3 minutes
	tail and middle cut	5-6 minutes per 500g (1lb)	**Skate**		5-6 minutes
Halibut	steaks and fillets	4-6 minutes	**Sole**	fillets	4-6 minutes
	tail and middle cut	5-6 minutes per 500g (1lb)		whole	5-6 minutes per 500g (1lb)
Herrings	filleted	4-5 minutes	**Trout**		6 minutes per 500g (1lb)
	whole	5-8 minutes	**Turbot**		5-6 minutes per 500g (1lb)
Lobster		10 minutes	**Whiting**	filleted	4-5 minutes
Mackerel	filleted	4-5 minutes		whole	5-8 minutes per 500g (1lb)
	whole	5-8 minutes			
Mullet	filleted	4-5 minutes			
	whole	5-8 minutes			

FISH

SOUSED MACKEREL

8 servings
6 minutes HIGH pressure

Metric/Imperial

1 litre (1¾ pints) dry white wine
2 carrots, scraped and thinly sliced
2 medium-sized onions, peeled and thinly sliced
8 mackerel, filleted and rolled with the skin on the outside
4 teaspoons chopped fresh marjoram or 2 teaspoons dried marjoram
2 whole cloves
4 bay leaves
1 teaspoon black peppercorns
1 teaspoon allspice berries
1 teaspoon salt
1 lemon, sliced

American

4 cups dry white wine
2 carrots, scraped and thinly sliced
2 medium-sized onions, peeled and thinly sliced
8 mackerel, filleted and rolled with the skin on the outside
4 teaspoons chopped fresh marjoram or 2 teaspoons dried marjoram
2 whole cloves
4 bay leaves
1 teaspoon black peppercorns
1 teaspoon allspice berries
1 teaspoon salt
1 lemon, sliced

Remove the trivet. Pour the wine into the cooker and add the carrots and onions. Bring to the boil in the open cooker over moderate heat. Reduce the heat to low and simmer the liquid for 10 minutes.

Remove the cooker from the heat and pour the liquid through a strainer placed over a large bowl. Discard the contents of the strainer and reserve the liquid.

Arrange the fillets in the cooker. Pour over the reserved liquid and sprinkle over the marjoram, cloves, bay leaves, peppercorns, allspice and salt. Bring to HIGH pressure and cook for 6 minutes.

If serving hot, reduce the pressure with cold water. Using a slotted spoon, transfer the fish to a warmed serving dish. Set aside and keep hot.

Boil the liquid rapidly in the open cooker over high heat until it is reduced by half. Strain the liquid over the fish, decorate with the lemon slices and serve immediately.

If serving cold, allow the pressure to reduce at room temperature. Leave the fish in the cooker until it is quite cold. When it has cooled completely, using a slotted spoon, transfer the fish to a serving dish. Set aside.

Place the open cooker over moderate heat and bring to the boil. Increase the

heat to high and boil the liquid rapidly until it has reduced by about half. Allow the liquid to cool completely and then pour it through a strainer over the fish. Decorate with the lemon slices and serve.

Fresh mackerel cooked in wine and spices, Soused Mackerel makes an ideal supper dish for the family, (especially if you catch them yourself), or for a buffet party. Either way serve it with lots of salad and brown bread and butter.

MIXED SEAFOOD CASSEROLE

8 servings
8 minutes HIGH pressure

Metric/Imperial

225g (8oz) canned crabmeat, cartilage and shell removed
1 egg, lightly beaten
1 tablespoon chopped fresh parsley
½ teaspoon salt
½ teaspoon black pepper
8 sole fillets, skinned
450g (1lb) shrimps, shelled
225g (8oz) scallops, halved
125ml (4fl oz) fish stock
125ml (4fl oz) dry white wine
50ml (2fl oz) lemon juice
150ml (5fl oz) double cream
1 lemon, cut into wedges

American

8 oz canned crabmeat, cartilage and shell removed
1 egg, lightly beaten
1 tablespoon chopped fresh parsley
½ teaspoon salt
½ teaspoon black pepper
8 sole fillets
1lb cooked shrimps, shelled
½lb scallops
½ cup fish stock
½ cup dry white wine
¼ cup lemon juice
⅔ cup heavy cream
1 lemon, cut into wedges

In a small bowl, mash the crabmeat with a fork. Add the egg, parsley, salt and pepper and mix to a smooth paste.

Spread the paste thickly over one side of each of the sole fillets. Roll up the fillets.

Remove the trivet from the cooker. Place the fish rolls in the cooker. Arrange the shrimps and scallops over and around the rolls. Pour in the fish stock, wine and lemon juice. Bring to HIGH pressure and cook for 8 minutes.

Reduce the pressure with cold water.

Using a slotted spoon, transfer the fish rolls and the shellfish to a warmed serving dish. Keep warm while you make the sauce.

Bring the liquid to the boil in the open cooker. Boil rapidly for 3 minutes or until the liquid had reduced by about half. Reduce the heat to low and add the cream. Cook the sauce, stirring constantly, for 2 to 3 minutes, or until it is hot but not boiling.

Remove the cooker from the heat and pour the sauce over the fish rolls and the shellfish. Garnish with the lemon wedges and serve immediately.

SALMON
with HOLLANDAISE SAUCE

4 servings
6 minutes HIGH pressure

Metric/Imperial

4 salmon steaks
300ml (½ pint) water
1 carrot, scraped and cut into 3cm (1in) lengths
1 celery stalk, trimmed and cut into 3cm (1in) lengths
2 shallots or small onions, halved
6 peppercorns
bouquet garni consisting of 4 parsley sprigs, 1 thyme spray and 1 bay leaf tied together
1 teaspoon salt
4 parsley sprigs
SAUCE
5 tablespoons white wine vinegar
6 peppercorns
1 bay leaf
175g (6oz) butter
3 egg yolks
¼ teaspoon salt

American

4 salmon steaks
1¼ cups water
1 carrot, scraped and cut into 1in lengths
1 celery stalk, trimmed and cut into 1in lengths
2 shallots or small onions, halved
6 peppercorns
bouquet garni, consisting of 4 parsley sprigs, 1 thyme spray and 1 bay leaf tied together
1 teaspoon salt
4 parsley sprigs
SAUCE
5 tablespoons white wine vinegar
6 peppercorns
1 bay leaf
1½ sticks butter
3 egg yolks
¼ teaspoon salt

Wash the salmon steaks in cold water

and dry with kitchen paper towels.

Remove the trivet from the pressure cooker and arrange the salmon steaks in the cooker. Pour over the water and add the carrot, celery, shallots or small onions, peppercorns, bouquet garni and salt. Bring to HIGH pressure and cook for 6 minutes.

Reduce the pressure with cold water.

Using a slotted spoon, transfer the salmon steaks to a warmed serving dish. Keep warm while you prepare the sauce.

Put the vinegar, peppercorns and bay leaf in a small saucepan and bring to the boil over moderate heat. Reduce the heat to moderately low and simmer the mixture for 10 minutes, or until it is reduced to 1¼ tablespoons. Pour the vinegar mixture through a strainer into a cup. Set aside. Discard the peppercorns and the bay leaf.

In a small mixing bowl, cream the butter with a wooden spoon until it is soft. In another small, heatproof mixing bowl, beat the egg yolks with a wire whisk or wooden spoon to blend them together. Beat in the salt and a heaped teaspoon of the softened butter. Stir in the strained vinegar.

Fill a medium-sized saucepan one-third full with warm water. Put the bowl with the egg yolk mixture into it. Place the pan over very low heat. The water should heat gradually but never come to boiling point. Stir the egg yolk mixture until it begins to thicken.

Add the remaining butter, a teaspoon at a time, stirring constantly. When all the butter has been added, taste the sauce. Add a little more salt if necessary. If the sauce is too sharp, add a little more butter. If the sauce is too thick, add 1 to 2 tablespoons of cream to dilute it.

Pour the sauce into a warmed sauceboat and serve with the salmon steaks, garnished with the parsley sprigs.

SALT COD STEW

4-6 servings
10-12 minutes HIGH pressure

Metric/Imperial

1kg (2lb) salt cod
25g (1oz) butter
2 tablespoons olive oil
2 large onions, peeled and chopped

600ml (1 pint) hot milk
1 teaspoon black pepper
4 tablespoons finely chopped fresh parsley
2 tablespoons double cream
1 tablespoon beurre manié, made by blending 1 tablespoon butter with 2 tablespoons flour

American

2lb salt cod
2 tablespoons butter
2 tablespoons olive oil
2 large onions, peeled and chopped
1¼ cups hot milk
1 teaspoon black pepper
4 tablespoons finely chopped fresh parsley
2 tablespoons heavy cream
1 tablespoon beurre manié, made by blending 1 tablespoon butter with 2 tablespoons flour

Place the cod in a medium-sized mixing bowl and pour over enough cold water to cover. Set aside for 24 hours, changing the water twice.

Remove the cod from the water and rinse well. Pat the fish dry with kitchen paper towels and set aside.

Remove the trivet from the pressure cooker. Melt the butter with the oil over moderate heat. When the foam subsides, add the onions and fry, stirring occasionally, for 5 to 7 minutes or until they are soft and translucent but not brown. Add the fish and fry for 5 minutes, turning once.

Pour over the milk and add the pepper and the parsley. Bring to HIGH pressure and cook for 10 to 12 minutes.

Reduce the pressure with cold water.

Using a slotted spoon, transfer the fish to a warmed serving dish. Keep warm while you prepare the sauce.

Stir the cream into the cooking liquid in the open cooker over low heat. Add the beurre manié, a little at a time, beating it well into the sauce. Cook, stirring constantly, for a further 2 minutes or until the sauce is fairly thick and smooth.

Pour the sauce over the fish and serve immediately.

Right : Salt Cod Stew is an unusual dish which probably originated in the Virgin Islands, but which is known all over the West Indies.

HADDOCK with MUSTARD SAUCE

4 servings
5 minutes HIGH pressure

Metric/Imperial

8 haddock fillets
50g (2oz) flour
150g (5oz) butter, melted
150ml (5fl oz) milk
150ml (5fl oz) single cream
2 teaspoons prepared English mustard
½ teaspoon salt
½ teaspoon white pepper

American

8 haddock fillets
½ cup flour
10 tablespoons butter, melted
⅔ cup light cream
2 teaspoons prepared English mustard
½ teaspoon salt
½ teaspoon white pepper

Remove the trivet from the pressure cooker.

Coat the haddock fillets with the flour and dip them in about two-thirds of the butter.

Heat the remaining butter in the open cooker over moderate heat. Place the

fillets in the cooker and pour over the milk and cream. Bring to HIGH pressure and cook for 5 minutes.

Reduce the pressure with cold water.

Transfer the fillets to a warmed serving dish and keep hot while you prepare the sauce.

Place the open cooker over moderate heat and add the mustard, salt and pepper to the cooking liquid, stirring well to blend. Increase the heat to high and boil, stirring constantly, until the sauce has thickened slightly.

Remove the cooker from the heat, pour the sauce over the fish and serve immediately.

PLAICE with ARTICHOKE SAUCE

4 servings
4 minutes HIGH pressure

Metric/Imperial

1kg (2lb) plaice fillets
1 teaspoon salt
1 teaspoon black pepper
1 small onion, peeled and pushed out into rings
1 celery stalk, trimmed and chopped
1 mace blade
bouquet garni, consisting of 4 parsley sprigs, 1 thyme spray and 1 bay leaf tied together
6 white peppercorns, crushed
300ml (10fl oz) water or fish stock
175ml (6fl oz) dry white wine
1 tablespoon lemon juice
1 tablespoon chopped fresh parsley
SAUCE
25g (1oz) butter
25g (1oz) flour
¼ teaspoon salt
⅛ teaspoon white pepper
⅛ teaspoon cayenne pepper
50ml (2fl oz) double cream
6 artichoke hearts, cooked, drained and chopped

American

2lb flounder fillets
1 teaspoon salt
1 teaspoon black pepper
1 small onion, peeled and pushed out into rings
1 celery stalk, trimmed and chopped
1 mace blade
bouquet garni, consisting of 4 parsley sprigs, 1 thyme spray and 1 bay leaf tied together
6 white peppercorns, crushed
1¼ cups water or fish stock

Above : Plaice [Flounder] with Artichoke Sauce is very quick to prepare.

¾ cup dry white wine
1 tablespoon lemon juice
1 tablespoon chopped fresh parsley
SAUCE
2 tablespoons butter
4 tablespoons flour
¼ teaspoon salt
⅛ teaspoon white pepper
⅛ teaspoon cayenne pepper
¼ cup heavy cream
6 artichoke hearts, cooked, drained and chopped

Put the fish fillets on a working surface and rub them all over with the salt and pepper.

Remove the trivet from the cooker and arrange the fillets on the bottom of the cooker. Add the onion, celery, mace blade, bouquet garni and peppercorns. Pour over the water or fish stock and the wine and add the lemon juice. Bring to HIGH pressure and cook for 4 minutes.

Reduce the pressure with cold water. Using a slotted spoon, transfer the fish to a warmed serving dish. Keep warm while you make the sauce.

Pour the cooking liquid through a

fine wire strainer over a bowl. Discard the contents of the strainer.

In a large frying-pan, melt the butter over moderate heat. Remove the pan from the heat and, with a wooden spoon, stir in the flour to make a smooth paste. Gradually add 300ml (10fl oz) [1¼ cups] of the strained cooking liquid, stirring constantly. Return the pan to the heat and cook, stirring constantly, for 2 to 3 minutes, or until the sauce is thick and smooth.

Remove the pan from the heat. Stir in the salt, pepper and cayenne. Stir in the cream and then the artichoke heart pieces. Taste the sauce and add more salt and pepper, if necessary. Pour the sauce over the fish fillets, sprinkle with parsley and serve immediately.

RAIE AU BEURRE NOIR

6 servings
3 minutes HIGH pressure
6 minutes HIGH pressure

Metric/Imperial

COURT BOUILLON
400ml (¾ pint) water or water and wine mixed
125g (¼lb) carrots, scraped and sliced
1 small onion, sliced
1 celery stalk, chopped
bouquet garni, consisting of 4 parsley sprigs, 1 thyme spray and 1 bay leaf tied together
4 peppercorns
½ teaspoon salt
50ml (2fl oz) cider or wine vinegar
2kg (4lb) skate wings, cleaned and trimmed
BEURRE NOIR
175g (6oz) butter
3 tablespoons chopped parsley
4 tablespoons wine vinegar or lemon juice
¼ teaspoon salt
¼ teaspoon black pepper

American

COURT BOUILLON
2 cups water or water and wine mixed
¼lb carrots, scraped and sliced
1 small onion, sliced
1 celery stalk, chopped
bouquet garni, consisting of 4 parsley sprigs, 1 thyme spray and 1 bay leaf tied together
4 peppercorns
½ teaspoon salt
¼ cup cider or wine vinegar
4lb skate wings, cleaned and trimmed
BEURRE NOIR
¾ cup butter
3 tablespoons chopped parsley
4 tablespoons wine vinegar or lemon juice
¼ teaspoon salt
¼ teaspoon black pepper

First make the court bouillon. Remove the trivet. Pour the water or mixed water and wine into the cooker. Add the carrots, onion, celery, bouquet garni, peppercorns, salt and vinegar. Place the open cooker over high heat and bring the liquid to the boil. Bring to HIGH pressure and cook for 3 minutes.

Allow the pressure to reduce at room temperature.

Strain the liquid through cheesecloth or a fine strainer into a large bowl. Discard the contents of the strainer.

Arrange the skate wings in the cooker. Pour over the strained court bouillon. Bring to HIGH pressure and cook for 6 minutes.

Reduce the pressure with cold water.

Meanwhile, make the beurre noir. Clarify the butter by cutting it into small pieces and placing them in a saucepan over moderately low heat. When the butter has melted, skim off the foam and pour the clear, remaining butter into a bowl. Discard the milky residue at the bottom of the pan. Rinse the pan and strain the butter into it.

Place the pan over moderate heat. When the butter has turned a golden, nut-brown, remove the pan from the heat and stir in the parsley. Pour the mixture into a bowl.

Pour the vinegar or lemon juice into the same saucepan and boil it over a moderately high heat until it has reduced to one tablespoon. Stir the liquid into the browned butter. Add the salt and pepper to the mixture.

Place the bowl over hot water to keep warm.

Using a slotted spoon, transfer the fish to a wooden board. Discard the cooking liquid. Using a sharp knife, remove the skin and cut the fish into 5cm (2in) strips.

Place the fish on a warmed serving dish. Pour over the hot beurre noir and serve immediately.

HALIBUT STUFFED with SHRIMPS

6 servings
20 minutes HIGH pressure

Metric/Imperial

125g (4oz) canned crabmeat
50g (2oz) plus 1 teaspoon butter
225g (8oz) shrimps, shelled
2 tablespoons flour
225ml (8fl oz) fish stock
50ml (2fl oz) double cream
50ml (2fl oz) dry white wine
125g (4oz) mushrooms, wiped clean and chopped
1 small green pepper, white pith removed, seeded and chopped
50g (2oz) cooked rice
½ teaspoon salt
¼ teaspoon black pepper
1 × 1.5kg (1 × 3lb) tail end of halibut, centre bone removed
300ml (10fl oz) water
parsley sprigs
lemon wedges

American

4oz canned crabmeat
4 tablespoons plus 1 teaspoon butter
½lb cooked shrimps, shelled
2 tablespoons flour
1 cup fish stock
¼ cup heavy cream
¼ cup dry white wine
¼lb mushrooms, wiped clean and chopped
¾ cup cooked rice
½ teaspoon salt
¼ teaspoon black pepper
1 x 3lb tail end of halibut, centre bone removed
1¼ cups water
parsley sprigs
lemon wedges

Remove any shell and cartilage from the crabmeat and set aside.

Melt the 50g (2oz) [4 tablespoons] butter in a large frying pan over moderate heat. When the foam subsides, reduce the heat to low and add the crabmeat and shrimps to the pan, stirring well until they are well coated with butter. Stir in the flour.

Above: Halibut stuffed with shrimps and crabmeat is a truely sumptuous seafood dinner party dish.

Pour in the fish stock, cream and wine, stirring constantly until they are well blended. Heat gently until the liquid is hot but not boiling.

Add the mushrooms, green pepper, rice, salt and pepper, stirring constantly. Remove the pan from the heat and spoon the crabmeat mixture into the pocket of the halibut.

Lightly grease a rectangle of greaseproof or waxed paper. Wrap the fish in it, enclosing any excess crabmeat mixture and making a firm, but not tight parcel. Remove the trivet and pour the water into the pressure cooker. Replace the trivet and arrange the fish on it. Bring to HIGH pressure and cook for 20 minutes.

Reduce the pressure with cold water.

Transfer the fish to a warmed serving dish, using two large spoons, and unwrap the parcel. Garnish with the parsley sprigs and lemon wedges and serve immediately.

COD, SPANISH-STYLE

4 servings
5 minutes HIGH pressure

Metric/Imperial

3 tablespoons olive oil
1 small onion, peeled and finely
  chopped
2 large garlic cloves, crushed
50g (2oz) ground almonds
12g (½oz) fresh breadcrumbs
4 tablespoons chopped fresh parsley
500g (1lb) tomatoes, blanched, peeled,
  seeded and chopped
1kg (2lb) cod fillets
300ml (½ pint) hot water
juice of ½ lemon
½ teaspoon salt
bouquet garni, consisting of 4 parsley
  sprigs, 1 thyme spray, 1 bay leaf tied
  together
6 black peppercorns tied in a piece of
  muslin
2 tablespoons blanched, flaked
  almonds

American

3 tablespoons olive oil
1 small onion, peeled and finely
  chopped
2 large garlic cloves, crushed
½ cup ground almonds
¼ cup fresh breadcrumbs
4 tablespoons chopped fresh parsley
1lb tomatoes, blanched, peeled,
  seeded and chopped
2lb cod fillets
1¼ cups hot water
juice of ½ lemon
½ teaspoon salt
bouquet garni, consisting of 4 parsley
  sprigs, 1 thyme spray and 1 bay leaf
  tied together
6 black peppercorns, tied in a piece of
  cheesecloth
2 tablespoons blanched, flaked
  almonds

In a large frying-pan, heat the oil over moderate heat. When it is hot, add the onion and garlic and cook, stirring occasionally, for 5 to 7 minutes or until the onion is soft and translucent, but not brown.

Remove the pan from the heat and stir in the ground almonds, breadcrumbs, 3 tablespoons of the parsley and the tomatoes. Return the pan to the heat and cook, stirring constantly, for 5 minutes or until the liquid in the pan has evaporated and the mixture is thick. Remove the pan from the heat and set aside.

Remove the trivet from the cooker. Arrange the fillets on the bottom of the cooker and pour over the hot water and the lemon juice. Add the salt, the bouquet garni and the peppercorns. Bring to HIGH pressure and cook for 5 minutes.

Reduce the pressure with cold water.

Using a slotted spoon, transfer the fillets to a warmed serving dish. Cover with aluminium foil to keep them warm while you prepare the sauce.

Strain and reserve 75ml (3fl oz) [⅓ cup] of the fish cooking liquid. Add it to the tomato and almond mixture in the frying pan, stirring well to blend. Place the pan over moderate heat and cook, stirring constantly, until the mixture is smooth.

Remove and discard the aluminium foil from the fish. Pour the sauce over the fish and sprinkle with the flaked almonds and the remaining parsley. Serve immediately.

KEDGEREE

4 servings
5 minutes HIGH pressure

Metric/Imperial

150ml (¼ pint) water
2 eggs
225g (8oz) long grain rice
400ml (15fl oz) salted water
50g (2oz) butter
350g (12oz) smoked haddock
1 teaspoon salt
½ teaspoon black pepper
½ teaspoon cayenne pepper
2 tablespoons single cream
1 tablespoon chopped fresh parsley

American

1¼ cups water
2 eggs
1¼ cups long grain rice
2 cups salted water
4 tablespoons butter
¾lb smoked haddock
1 teaspoon salt
½ teaspoon black pepper
½ teaspoon cayenne pepper
2 tablespoons light cream
1 tablespoon chopped fresh parsley

Remove the trivet from the cooker. Pour in the water and add the eggs. Put the rice and salted water in the unperforated container. Use one teaspoon of butter to grease a piece of greaseproof or waxed paper and cover the unperforated container. Place the container in the cooker. Place the trivet on top.

Put the haddock on the trivet and dot one teaspoon of butter over the fish. Cover with greaseproof paper. Bring to HIGH pressure, and cook for 5 minutes.

Allow the pressure to reduce at room temperature.

Using two large spoons, transfer the fish to a working surface. Set aside until it is cool enough to handle. Turn the rice into a large frying-pan and place the eggs in cold water.

Using a sharp knife, remove the skin and bones from the haddock and flake the fish. Peel and finely chop the hard boiled eggs.

Place the frying-pan over very low heat and shake it gently for 1 minute or until the rice is dry and fluffy. Add the remaining butter, the flaked fish, chopped eggs, salt, pepper and cayenne. Increase the heat to moderate and stir in the cream.

Heat the kedgeree for 3 to 5 minutes or until it is hot. Remove the pan from the heat and pile the mixture on to a warmed serving dish. Garnish with the parsley and serve immediately.

Kedgeree is the traditional English country house breakfast dish, which would probably have been part of a choice including devilled kidneys and perfect scrambled eggs, followed by hot buttered toast and old-fashioned, thick-cut marmalade. Nowadays kedgeree stands on its own at any time of day.

FISH

SCALLOPS IN CREAM SAUCE

4 servings
5 minutes HIGH pressure

Metric/Imperial

150ml (5fl oz) white wine
150ml (5fl oz) fish stock
1 teaspoon lemon juice
500g (1lb) scallops
1 tablespoon butter
2 tablespoons flour
150ml (5fl oz) single cream
¼ teaspoon salt
¼ teaspoon black pepper
⅛ teaspoon cayenne pepper
25g (1oz) Gruyère cheese, grated

American

⅔ cup white wine
⅔ cup fish stock
1 teaspoon lemon juice
1lb scallops
1 tablespoon butter
2 tablespoons flour
⅔ cup light cream
¼ teaspoon black pepper
⅛ teaspoon cayenne pepper
¼ cup Gruyère cheese, grated

Remove the trivet from the pressure cooker and pour in the wine and fish stock. Add the lemon juice and the scallops. Bring to HIGH pressure and cook for 5 minutes.

Allow the pressure to reduce at room temperature.

Set on one side to cool.

When the liquid has cooled, strain it into a bowl and set aside.

With a sharp knife, slice the scallops in half if they are large. Set aside.

Melt the butter in the open cooker over low heat. Remove the cooker from the heat and, with a wooden spoon, stir in the flour. Gradually add 125ml (4fl oz) [½ cup] of the reserved cooking liquid, stirring constantly. Return the pan to moderate heat and bring the sauce to the boil. Cook the sauce for 4 minutes, stirring constantly. Stir in the cream, salt, pepper, cayenne and cook for a further 2 minutes. Fold the scallops into the sauce.

Preheat the grill [broiler].

Spoon the scallops and sauce into 4 large scallop shells or individual cocotte dishes. Sprinkle the grated Gruyère over the tops. Brown under the grill [broiler] for 4 to 5 minutes. Serve immediately.

Below : Scallops in cream sauce look interesting in individual dishes with mashed potatoes piped round the edge.

SOLE BONNE FEMME

6 servings
5 minutes HIGH pressure

Metric/Imperial

½ teaspoon salt
½ teaspoon black pepper
800g (1½in) sole fillets, skinned
125g (4oz) button mushrooms, wiped clean and chopped
2 shallots, finely chopped
150ml (5fl oz) dry white wine
150ml (5fl oz) fish stock
1 tablespoon lemon juice
bouquet garni, consisting of 4 parsley sprigs, 1 thyme spray and 1 bay leaf tied together
25g (1oz) butter
2 tablespoons flour
2 tablespoons double cream
12 mushroom caps, sautéed in 25g (1oz) butter

American

½ teaspoon salt
½ teaspoon black pepper
1½lb sole fillets
¼lb button mushrooms, wiped clean and chopped
2 shallots, finely chopped
⅔ cup dry white wine

⅔ cup fish stock

1 tablespoon lemon juice

bouquet garni, consisting of 4 parsley sprigs, 1 thyme spray and 1 bay leaf tied together

2 tablespoons butter

2 tablespoons flour

2 tablespoons heavy cream

12 mushroom caps, sautéed in 2 tablespoons butter

Rub the salt and pepper on the fillets and set aside.

Remove the trivet from the cooker. Arrange the mushrooms and shallots over the bottom of the cooker. Replace the trivet and place the fish fillets on it

(they may be folded in half if necessary) Pour over the wine, fish stock and lemon juice and add the bouquet garni. Bring to HIGH pressure and cook for 5 minutes.

Reduce the pressure with cold water.

Remove and discard the bouquet garni. Using a slotted spoon, transfer the fish to a warmed serving dish. Set aside and keep warm while you finish the sauce.

Pour the cooking liquid through a strainer set over a large mixing bowl, pressing down hard on the vegetables with the back of a wooden spoon. Discard the contents of the strainer and reserve the liquid for later use.

Above : Sole Bonne Femme is a classic fish dish with button mushrooms.

Melt the butter in the open cooker over moderate heat. Remove the cooker from the heat, and, using a wooden spoon, stir in the flour to make a smooth paste. Gradually add the reserved cooking liquid, stirring constantly until the sauce is smooth. Return the cooker to low heat and cook the sauce, stirring constantly, for 2 to 3 minutes or until it is thick and smooth. Stir in the cream and remove the cooker from the heat.

Pour the sauce over the fish and arrange the mushroom caps around the fish to garnish. Serve immediately.

MEAT

Meat dishes are probably the most important and the most expensive part of the day's meals and it is with these that the pressure cooker demonstrates its true worth.

As well as being economical, cheaper cuts of meat usually have a great nutritional value and more flavour than expensive ones. The speed of pressure cooking and the tenderizing effect make this an ideal method for preparing stews, casseroles, pot roasts and an immense variety of tasty and appetizing dishes.

General hints

Small cuts of meat, such as chops, should have excess fat trimmed off before cooking.

Be careful not to overcook the meat. Every extra minute of cooking under pressure is equivalent to about 10 minutes of ordinary cooking and can result in stringy, tasteless meat. Some variation in cooking time is given in the recipes which follow. The weight, size, thickness, quality and the proportions of fat, lean and bone will all have some effect. You will quickly acquire enough experience to judge how long the cooking time should be to achieve exactly the texture and taste you require. If you are adapting the recipes for fewer or for more servings, it is important to remember that the pressure cooking time will not change for meat cut into cubes, chops or even-sized pieces. It is only necessary to adjust the cooking times for roasts, which are timed according to their weight. Roasts up to $1\frac{1}{2}$kg (3lb) are the most suitable for large cookers and proportionately smaller ones should be used in smaller cookers. They should be positioned as centrally as possible to allow plenty of room for the steam to circulate for thorough and even cooking.

As the cooking time is so short, very little liquid is lost through evaporation. The gravy will be concentrated and to ensure the right consistency, it is best to reduce and thicken it in the open cooker after cooking. The liquid can be stock, water, cider, beer, wine or a variety of sauces. The meat should be cooked in just enough liquid for serving in the case of stews and casseroles, with a minimum quantity of liquid under the trivet for pot roasts and with the cooker half full for boiling bacon or ham. A general guide is 300ml ($\frac{1}{2}$ pint) [$1\frac{1}{4}$ cups] of liquid for the first 15 to 20 minutes of the cooking time and an extra 150ml ($\frac{1}{4}$ pint) [$\frac{1}{2}$ cup] for every extra 15 minutes cooking time.

Receipes often require meat to be browned in hot oil or fat to seal in the juices before cooking. The surplus oil should be drained off and the liquid should be heated before it is added to the pressure cooker. Otherwise, too much liquid can be lost as steam when cold liquid is poured into a hot cooker. It is not necessary to thaw frozen meat before cooking unless it has to be browned in hot oil first. To reheat cooked stews and casseroles from the freezer, remove the trivet and pour 150ml ($\frac{1}{4}$ pint) [$\frac{1}{2}$ cup] water or stock into the cooker. Transfer the frozen food from its packaging to the cooker and bring to HIGH pressure. Cook for 2 to 4 minutes and reduce the pressure at room temperature.

Left : Meat isn't getting any cheaper, so a pressure cooker is a boon. It makes delicious stews in very little time from inexpensive cuts, and locks in all the goodness as well.

General guide to cooking times (HIGH pressure)

Boiling and Pickling (without trivet), cooker half-full

Bacon	12-15 minutes per 500g (1lb)	Pork (plain)	12 minutes
Beef	15-20 minutes per 500g (1lb)	Pork (stuffed)	12-15 minutes
Ham	12-15 minutes per 500g (1lb)	Veal (plain)	12 minutes
Mutton	15 minutes per 500g (1lb)	Veal (stuffed)	12-15 minutes
Pig's head	40-45 minutes		
Pig's trotters	30 minutes	**Pot Roasts (with trivet)**	
Pork	18-20 minutes per 500g (1lb)	Beef	12-18 minutes per 500g (1lb)
		Lamb	10-15 minutes per 500g (1lb)
Braising (without trivet)		Mutton	10-15 minutes per 500g (1lb)
		Pork	15-18 minutes per 500g (1lb)
Beef	15-20 minutes	Veal	12-15 minutes per 500g (1lb)
Gammon [Ham]	10 minutes		
Heart	40 minutes	**Stewing (without trivet)**	
Kidneys	7 minutes		
Lamb	10 minutes	Beef	15-20 minutes
Liver	5 minutes	Lamb	10 minutes
Mutton	10 minutes	Pork	12-15 minutes
Oxtail	40 minutes	Veal	12-15 minutes

BOEUF BOURGUIGNONNE

6-8 servings
15 minutes HIGH pressure
3 minutes HIGH pressure

Metric/Imperial

175g (6oz) streaky bacon, in
   one piece
1 tablespoon olive oil
1.25kg (3lb) lean beef, cut into 5cm
   (2in) cubes
1 carrot, scraped and sliced
1 onion, peeled and sliced
1 teaspoon salt
¼ teaspoon black pepper
4 tablespoons flour
300ml (½ pint) hot beef stock
600ml (1 pint) dry red wine
1 tablespoon tomato paste
3 garlic cloves, crushed
½ teaspoon thyme
1 bay leaf
2 tablespoons chopped parsley
ONIONS
1½ tablespoons butter
1 tablespoon vegetable oil
18 small onions, peeled
300ml (½ pint) beef stock or beef stock
   and red wine
bouquet garni, consisting of 4 parsley
   sprigs, 1 thyme spray and 1 bay leaf
   tied together
¼ teaspoon salt
¼ teaspoon white pepper
MUSHROOMS
2 teaspoons vegetable oil
500g (1lb) button mushrooms, wiped
   clean

American

6oz bacon, in one piece
1 tablespoon olive oil
3lb lean beef, cut into 2in cubes
1 carrot, scraped and sliced
1 onion, peeled and sliced
1 teaspoon salt
¼ teaspoon black pepper
4 tablespoons flour
1¼ cups hot beef stock
2½ cups dry red wine
1 tablespoon tomato paste
3 garlic cloves, crushed
½ teaspoon thyme
1 bay leaf
2 tablespoons chopped parsley
ONIONS
1½ tablespoons butter
1 tablespoon vegetable oil
18 small onions, peeled
1¼ cups beef stock or beef stock and
   red wine
bouquet garni, consisting of 4 parsley
   sprigs, 1 thyme spray and 1 bay leaf
   tied together
¼ teaspoon salt
¼ teaspoon white pepper
MUSHROOMS
2 teaspoons vegetable oil
1lb button mushrooms, wiped clean

With a sharp knife, remove the rind
from the bacon. Cut the bacon into
strips 0.5cm (¼in) thick and 3cm (1½in)
long.

Remove the trivet from the cooker.
Place the bacon strips and the olive oil
in the open cooker and cook over
moderate heat for 3 minutes, turning
the bacon several times so that it browns
on both sides. Using a slotted spoon,
transfer the bacon to a plate and set
aside.

Add the beef cubes to the cooker, a
few at a time, and, stirring occasionally,
brown them quickly on all sides. As the
cubes brown, transfer them to the plate
with the bacon.

Add the carrot and the onion and
cook, stirring occasionally, for 5 minutes. Carefully pour away any excess
fat and return the beef and bacon to the
cooker. Stir in the salt and pepper.
Sprinkle the flour over the meat cubes
and toss them lightly with a wooden
spoon. Remove the cooker from the
heat. Gradually add the beef stock and
the wine, stirring constantly. Return
the cooker to the heat and stir in the
tomato paste, garlic, thyme and bay
leaf. Bring to HIGH pressure and cook
for 15 minutes.

Reduce the pressure with cold water.
Meanwhile, begin to prepare the
onions. Melt the butter with the oil in a
medium-sized frying-pan. When the
foam subsides, turn the heat to low and
add the onions. Cook, stirring occasionally, for 10 minutes, or until they are
brown on all sides. Set aside.

When the beef is cooked, pour it
through a strainer placed over a large
mixing bowl. Reserve the cooking
liquid. Discard the bay leaf. Transfer
the beef mixture to a warmed serving
dish and keep hot.

Rinse out the cooker and transfer the
onions to it (without the trivet). Place
the open cooker over moderate heat.

Pour in the beef stock or beef stock and
red wine. Add the bouquet garni, salt
and pepper. Bring to HIGH pressure
and cook for 3 minutes.

Reduce the pressure with cold water.
Meanwhile, prepare the mushrooms.
Add the oil to the medium-sized frying-
pan and place over moderate heat.
When the foam subsides, add the mushrooms and cook, shaking the pan gently
occasionally, for 5 minutes, or until the
mushrooms are lightly browned. Using
a slotted spoon, transfer them to the
dish with the beef. Stir to mix together and set aside. Keep warm while
the onions finish cooking.

When the onions are cooked, remove
and discard the bouquet garni. Transfer
the onions to the dish with the beef and
mushrooms. Stir to mix. Keep warm
while you finish off the sauce.

Pour the reserved, strained liquid
into the open cooker and simmer over
moderate heat for 2 minutes. If the
sauce is too thin, boil it rapidly in the
open cooker to reduce and thicken it.
Pour the sauce over the meat and
vegetables. Sprinkle over the chopped
parsley and serve immediately.

LIVER, ITALIAN-STYLE

4 servings
4 minutes HIGH pressure

Metric/Imperial

125g (4oz) butter
2 shallots, finely chopped
2 garlic cloves, crushed
6 spring onions, finely chopped
125g (4oz) mushrooms, wiped clean
   and sliced
700g (1½lb) lamb's liver, thickly sliced
   and cut into 8cm (3in) pieces
400g (14oz) canned, peeled tomatoes,
   can juice reserved
2 tablespoons tomato purée
150ml (15fl oz) hot beef stock
½ tablespoon wine vinegar
½ teaspoon salt
¼ teaspoon black pepper
½ teaspoon dried thyme
½ teaspoon dried basil
1 bay leaf
1 tablespoon chopped fresh parsley

American

1 stick butter

2 shallots, finely chopped
2 garlic cloves, crushed
6 green onions, finely chopped
¼lb mushrooms, wiped clean and
 sliced
1½lb lamb's liver, thickly sliced and
 cut into 3in pieces
14oz can peeled tomatoes, can juice
 reserved
2 tablespoons tomato purée
2 cups hot beef stock
½ tablespoon wine vinegar
½ teaspoon salt
¼ teaspoon black pepper
½ teaspoon dried thyme
½ teaspoon dried basil
1 bay leaf
1 tablespoon chopped fresh parsley

Remove the trivet. Melt 50g (2oz) [4 tablespoons] of the butter over moderate heat. When the foam subsides, add the shallots, garlic and spring [green] onions and cook, stirring occasionally, for 3 to 5 minutes, or until the shallots are soft and translucent but not brown.

Add the mushrooms and cook, stirring occasionally for 4 minutes or until they are lightly browned.

Add the remaining butter to the open

cooker and melt over moderate heat. When the foam subsides, add the liver pieces, a few at a time, and cook them, stirring and turning occasionally, for 3 to 5 minutes or until they are lightly browned on all sides.

With a slotted spoon, transfer the cooked liver to a plate. Set aside.

Add the tomatoes and the can juice, tomatoe purée, stock and vinegar to the open cooker. Bring to the boil, stirring occasionally. Stir in the salt, pepper, thyme, basil, bay leaf and parsley and cook, stirring, for 1 minute. Return the liver to the cooker. Bring to HIGH pressure and cook for 4 minutes.

Reduce the pressure with cold water.

Remove and discard the bay leaf. Transfer the liver mixture to a warmed serving dish and serve immediately.

PORK CHOPS IN A PIQUANT SAUCE

6 servings
15 minutes HIGH pressure

Metric/Imperial

4 tablespoons olive oil
6 large pork chops, cut approximately
3cm (1in) thick
3 medium-sized onions, peeled and
 sliced
150ml (5fl oz) hot beef stock
150ml (5fl oz) dry white wine
1 tablespoon tomato purée
¼ teaspoon dried sage
¼ teaspoon dried rosemary
2 garlic cloves, crushed
½ teaspoon salt
¼ teaspoon black pepper
1 teaspoon prepared French mustard
1 medium-sized gherkin, sliced
1 teaspoon cornflour dissolved in 1
 tablespoon water
2 tablespoons chopped fresh parsley

American

4 tablespoons olive oil
6 large pork chops, cut approximately
 1in thick
3 medium-sized onions, peeled and
 sliced
⅔ cup hot beef stock
⅔ cup dry white wine
1 tablespoon tomato purée
¼ teaspoon dried sage
¼ teaspoon dried rosemary
2 garlic cloves, crushed
½ teaspoon salt
¼ teaspoon black pepper
1 teaspoon prepared French mustard
1 medium-sized gherkin, sliced
1 teaspoon cornstarch dissolved in
 1 tablespoon water
2 tablespoons chopped fresh parsley

Remove the trivet. Heat the oil in the open cooker over moderate heat. Add the chops, two or three at a time, and brown them on all sides. As the chops are browned, transfer them to a plate. Set aside and keep warm.

Add the onions and cook, stirring occasionally for 5 to 7 minutes, or until they are soft and translucent but not brown.

Pour in the beef stock and the wine. Add the tomato purée, sage, rosemary, garlic, salt and pepper. Stir until all the ingredients are thoroughly blended. Bring to the boil in the open cooker. Reduce the heat to low and simmer for 5 minutes.

Left: Liver, Italian-Style is a tasty combination of lambs liver, shallots, mushrooms and herbs — perfect for a quick, informal meal.

Stir in the mustard and add the pork chops. Bring to HIGH pressure and cook for 15 minutes.

Reduce the pressure with cold water.

With a slotted spoon, transfer the pork chops to a warmed serving dish. Set aside and keep warm while you finish off the sauce.

Bring the cooking liquid to the boil in the open cooker over high heat. Cook the sauce for 2 to 3 minutes, stirring frequently. Add the sliced gherkin and reduce the heat to moderate. Add the cornflour [cornstarch] mixture and cook, stirring constantly, for 2 minutes or until the sauce is thick.

Pour the sauce over the chops, sprinkle over the parsley and serve immediately.

STEAK AND KIDNEY PUDDING

4 servings
15 minutes pre-steaming
55 minutes LOW pressure

Metric/Imperial

DOUGH
225g (8oz) self-raising flour
¼ teaspoon salt
125g (4oz) suet, shredded
150ml (5fl oz) water
FILLING
2 teaspoons butter
500g (1lb) chuck steak, cut into small pieces
175g (6oz) kidney, cut into small pieces
1 tablespoon flour
¼ teaspoon salt
⅛ teaspoon black pepper
½ teaspoon dried thyme
150ml (5fl oz) beef stock
1½ litres (2½ pints) boiling water

American

DOUGH
2 cups self-raising cake flour
¼ teaspoon salt
¼lb shredded suet
⅔ cup water
FILLING
2 teaspoons butter
1lb chuck steak, cut into small pieces
6oz kidney, cut into small pieces
1 tablespoon flour
¼ teaspoon salt
⅛ teaspoon black pepper
½ teaspoon dried thyme

⅔ cup beef stock
6 cups boiling water

Sift the flour and salt together into a large mixing bowl. Rub in the suet with your fingertips. Gradually add the water and mix to make a soft dough. Turn the dough out on to a lightly floured board and knead with your hand until the dough is smooth and elastic.

With a floured rolling pin, roll out the dough into a large circle about 1cm (½in) thick. Cut a triangle (about one-third of the diameter) out of the circle and reserve it. Using 1 teaspoon of the butter, lightly grease a 1 litre (2 pint) pudding basin [1 quart round casserole]. Line the container with the large piece of dough. Dampen the edges and bring them together. Press the dough to the shape of the container and trim the top edges.

Put the beef and kidney pieces on a large plate and sprinkle over the flour salt, pepper and the thyme. Coat all the meat pieces with the flour mixture on all sides.

Put the meat into the lined container. Pour over the beef stock so that the dough case is approximately two-thirds full.

Lightly knead the reserved dough and the trimmings together. Roll out to a circle large enough to cover the container. Dampen the edges of the dough and place on top of the meat. Press the edges of the dough together to seal.

Cut out a circle of greaseproof or waxed paper about 10cm (4in) wider in diameter than the rim of the container. With the remaining butter, grease the paper circle. Cut out a circle of aluminium foil the same size. Put the 2 circles together with the buttered side of the greaseproof or waxed paper circle away from the foil, and, holding them firmly, make a 3cm (1in) pleat across the centre. Place the pleated paper and foil circles, foil uppermost, over the pudding. With a piece of string, securely tie the paper and foil circles around the rim of the basin, leaving a loop with which to lift the pudding out of the cooker when cooked.

Remove the trivet. Pour the boiling water into the pressure cooker. Replace the trivet. Place the pudding on the trivet and close the cooker but do not fit the indicator weight. Pre-steam over low heat for 15 minutes. This means

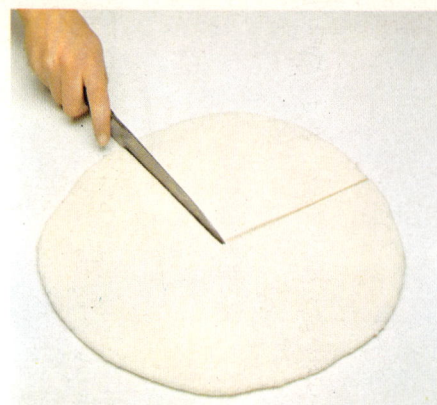

Roll out the dough into a large circle and cut a triangle out of it.

Line the basin with the pastry, bringing the cut edges together.

Lightly press the dough to the shape of the basin. Trim the edges.

Coat the beef and kidney pieces with flour, salt, pepper and herbs.

Put the meat into the lined basin and fill it two-thirds full with water.

Cover the bowl with aluminium foil and secure it with string.

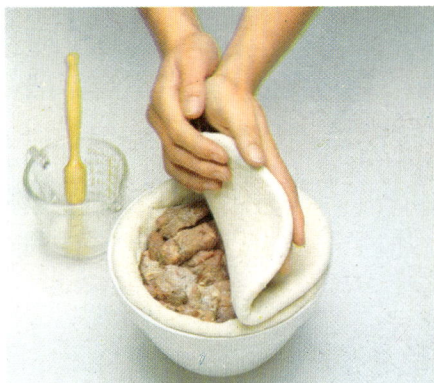

Place a circle of dough over the basin and press it into place.

Tie a piece of string over the top of the basin to form a handle.

that the water simmers and steam escapes through the vent.

Position the indicator weight. Bring to LOW pressure and cook for 55 minutes.

Allow the pressure to reduce at room temperature.

Lift the pudding out of the cooker. Remove the paper and foil circles. Serve, directly from the container immediately.

LAMB IN CIDER SAUCE

4 servings
10 minutes HIGH pressure

Metric/Imperial

8 lamb cutlets
1 teaspoon salt
½ teaspoon black pepper
1 garlic clove, halved
2 tablespoons oil
2 carrots, scraped and chopped
1 small turnip, peeled and quartered
1 leek, trimmed, washed and chopped
2 small onions, peeled and chopped
2 streaky bacon slices, chopped
½ teaspoon marjoram
300ml (10fl oz) hot chicken stock
300ml (10fl oz) still cider
50g (2oz) beurre manié, made by
    blending together 4 tablespoons
    butter with 8 tablespoons flour
⅛ teaspoon white pepper

American

8 lamb chops
1 teaspoon salt
½ teaspoon black pepper
1 garlic clove, halved
2 tablespoons oil
2 carrots, scraped and chopped
1 small turnip, peeled and quartered
1 leek, trimmed, washed and chopped
2 small onions, peeled and chopped
2 bacon slices, chopped
½ teaspoon marjoram
1¼ cups hot chicken stock
1¼ cups cider
4 tablespoons beurre manié, made by
    blending 4 tablespoons butter with
    8 tablespoons flour
⅛ teaspoon white pepper

Making a steak and kidney pudding is simple, if you follow these easy-to-follow steps and cook it in a pressure cooker.

Rub the lamb with ½ teaspoon of the salt, the pepper and the cut sides of the garlic. Set aside.

Remove the trivet. Pour in the oil and heat it in the open cooker over moderate heat. Place the meat in the open cooker and brown it for 3 minutes on each side.

Using a slotted spoon, remove the meat and set aside.

Place the carrots, turnip, leek, onions and bacon in the cooker. Fry them, stirring frequently, for 10 minutes.

Return the meat to the cooker and add the marjoram.

Pour over the stock and the cider. Bring to HIGH pressure and cook for 10 minutes.

Allow the pressure to reduce at room temperature.

Transfer the meat to a warmed serving dish. Set aside and keep warm while you prepare the sauce.

Pour the cooking liquid through a strainer placed over a medium-sized mixing bowl. Discard the contents of the strainer. Return the cooking liquid to the cooker. Place the open cooker over moderate heat and add the beurre manié a little at a time, stirring constantly, for a further 5 minutes, until the sauce is thick and smooth. Add the remaining salt and the white pepper.

Pour the sauce into a warmed sauce boat and serve separately with the lamb.

MEATBALL GOULASH

4 servings
15 minutes HIGH pressure
4 minutes HIGH pressure

Metric/Imperial

50ml (2fl oz) vegetable oil
2 medium-sized onions, peeled and finely chopped
1 garlic clove, crushed
2 carrots, scraped and sliced
125g (4oz) button mushrooms, wiped clean and thinly sliced
1 tablespoon paprika
150ml (5fl oz) hot beef stock
150ml (5fl oz) red wine
½ teaspoon salt
½ teaspoon black pepper
¼ teaspoon dried dill
½ teaspoon caraway seeds
4 large potatoes, peeled and quartered
2 teaspoons cornflour mixed with 1 tablespoon water
300ml (½ pint) sour cream

MEATBALLS

500g (1lb) minced beef
500g (1lb) minced pork
2 garlic cloves, crushed
½ teaspoon salt
½ teaspoon black pepper
½ teaspoon dried dill
¼ teaspoon cayenne pepper
4 slices rye bread, crusts removed and soaked for 5 minutes in 2 tablespoons milk
1 egg yolk
1 teaspoon grated orange rind

American

4 tablespoons vegetable oil
2 medium-sized onions, peeled and finely chopped
1 garlic clove, crushed
2 carrots, scraped and sliced
¼lb button mushrooms, wiped clean and thinly sliced
1 tablespoon paprika

Meatball Goulash is a piquant dish from Central Europe.

⅔ cup hot beef stock
⅔ cup red wine
½ teaspoon salt
½ teaspoon black pepper
¼ teaspoon dried dill
½ teaspoon caraway seeds
4 large potatoes, peeled and quartered
2 teaspoons cornstarch mixed with 1 tablespoon water
1 cup sour cream

MEATBALLS

1lb ground beef
1lb ground pork
2 garlic cloves, crushed
½ teaspoon salt
½ teaspoon black pepper
½ teaspoon dried dill
¼ teaspoon cayenne pepper
4 slices rye bread, crusts removed and soaked for 5 minutes in 2 tablespoons milk
1 egg yolk
1 teaspoon grated orange rind

First make the meatballs. In a large mixing bowl, beat all the meatball ingredients together until they are thoroughly blended. Using your hands, shape the mixture into small balls. Put all the balls on a large plate or baking sheet, cover them with foil or plastic wrap and put them in the refrigerator for 30 minutes to chill.

Heat the oil in the open cooker over moderate heat. When the oil is hot, add the onions, garlic and carrots and fry, stirring occasionally, for 5 to 7 minutes or until the onions are soft and translucent but not brown. Stir in the mushrooms and paprika and mix well. Fry the mixture, stirring occasionally, for a further 3 minutes. Pour in the stock and wine and add the salt, pepper dill and caraway seeds. Bring the liquid to the boil.

Remove the meatballs from the refrigerator and remove and discard the foil or plastic wrap. Add the meatballs to the cooker. Bring to HIGH pressure and cook for 15 minutes.

Reduce the pressure with cold water. Return the cooker to the heat. Add the potatoes. Bring to HIGH pressure and cook for 4 minutes.

Reduce the pressure with cold water. Return the cooker to the heat. Boil the liquid rapidly for 5 minutes over high heat. Reduce the heat to moderate and stir in the cornflour [cornstarch] mixture and the sour cream. Cook, stirring constantly, for a further 2 to 3 minutes, or until the sauce has thickened but is not boiling.

Transfer the mixture to a warmed serving dish and serve immediately.

ALOUETTES SANS TETES

4 servings
12 minutes HIGH pressure

Metric/Imperial

8 slices lean beef, each about 13cm
  (5in) square and
  0.5cm (¼in) thick
2 tablespoons cooking oil
2 onions, peeled and diced
2 carrots, scraped and diced
225g (8oz) tomatoes, blanched, peeled,
  seeded and sliced
1 clove garlic, crushed
1 bay leaf
600ml (1 pint) hot beef stock

2 tablespoons chopped fresh parsley
STUFFING
175g (6oz) minced pork or veal
1 small onion, peeled and finely
  chopped
25g (1oz) butter, softened
25g (1oz) fresh white breadcrumbs
1 tablespoon chopped fresh parsley
½ teaspoon dried sage
grated rind of 1 lemon
6 green olives, stoned and coarsely
  chopped
1 egg, lightly beaten
½ teaspoon salt
¼ teaspoon black pepper

American

8 slices lean beef, each about 5in
  square and ¼in thick
2 tablespoons cooking oil
2 onions, peeled and diced
2 carrots, scraped and diced
½lb tomatoes, blanched, peeled.
  seeded and sliced
1 clove garlic, crushed
1 bay leaf
2½ cups hot beef stock
2 tablespoons chopped fresh parsley
STUFFING
6oz ground pork or veal
1 small onion, peeled and finely
  chopped
2 tablespoons butter, softened
½ cup fresh white breadcrumbs
1 tablespoon chopped fresh parsley
½ teaspoon dried sage
grated rind of 1 lemon
6 green olives, pitted and coarsley
  chopped
1 egg, lightly beaten
½ teaspoon salt
¼ teaspoon black pepper

To prepare the stuffing, put the pork or veal, the onion, butter, breadcrumbs, parsley, sage, lemon rind and olives in a medium-sized mixing bowl. Using a fork, thoroughly combine the ingredients. Add the egg, salt and pepper and mix well to blend. Spread one-eighth of the stuffing on each slice of beef. Roll up the beef, tucking in the ends and tie with fine string.

Heat the oil in the open cooker over moderate heat. When the oil is hot, add the beef rolls, a few at a time and brown them on all sides. Using a slotted spoon, transfer them to a plate and keep warm.

Add the onions and carrots and cook,

stirring occasionally, for 8 minutes, or until the onions are golden brown.

Return the beef rolls to the cooker. Add the tomatoes, the garlic and the bay leaf. Pour over the stock and bring to HIGH pressure. Cook for 12 minutes.

Allow the pressure to reduce at room temperature.

Using a slotted spoon, transfer the beef rolls to a warmed serving dish. Carefully remove and discard the string. Pour the cooking liquid through a strainer over the beef rolls, pressing down hard on the vegetables with the back of a wooden spoon. Discard the contents of the strainer.

Sprinkle over the chopped parsley and serve immediately.

LAMB AND CASHEW NUT CURRY

4 servings
10 minutes HIGH pressure

Metric/Imperial

4cm (1½in) piece fresh root ginger,
  peeled and chopped
3 garlic cloves
2 green chillis
50g (2oz) unsalted cashew nuts
2 tablespoons water
4 cloves
¼ teaspoon cardamom seeds
1 tablespoon coriander seeds
1 tablespoon white poppy seeds
50g (2oz) butter
2 onions, peeled and chopped
1kg (2lb) boned leg or shoulder of
  lamb, cut into cubes
150ml (5fl oz) hot water
300ml (10fl oz) yogurt
¼ teaspoon saffron threads soaked in
  2 tablespoons boiling water or
  ¼ teaspoon ground saffron
½ teaspoon salt
juice of ¼ lemon
1 tablespoon chopped coriander leaves
1 lemon, sliced

American

1½in piece fresh root ginger, peeled
  and chopped
3 garlic cloves
2 green chilis
¾ cup unsalted cashew nuts
2 tablespoons water

4 cloves
$\frac{1}{4}$ teaspoon cardamom seeds
1 tablespoon coriander seeds
1 tablespoon white poppy seeds
4 tablespoons butter
2 onions, peeled and chopped
2lb boned leg or shoulder of lamb, cut
   into cubes
$\frac{2}{3}$ cup hot water
1 cup plain yogurt
$\frac{1}{4}$ teaspoon saffron threads, soaked in
   2 tablespoons boiling water or
   $\frac{1}{4}$ teaspoon ground saffron
$\frac{1}{2}$ teaspoon salt
juice of $\frac{1}{4}$ lemon
1 tablespoon chopped coriander
   leaves
1 lemon, sliced

Put the ginger, garlic, chillis, cashew nuts and the water in an electric blender. Blend at high speed until it forms a purée. Add the cloves, cardamom seeds, coriander seeds and poppy seeds. Blend at high speed.

Alternatively, put the ginger, garlic, chillis, cashew nuts, cardamom, coriander seeds, poppy seeds and water in a mortar and pound to a paste with a pestle.

Set the purée aside.

Remove the trivet. Melt the butter in the open cooker over moderate heat. When the foam subsides, add the onions and fry, stirring occasionally, for 8 to 10 minutes or until they are golden brown. Stir in the reserved spice purée.

Serve hot, spicy Lamb and Cashew Nut Curry with chappatis and chutney for an authentic Indian meal.

Reduce the heat to low and, stirring frequently, fry the purée for 3 minutes. Add the lamb cubes, increase the heat to moderately high and, tossing and turning the cubes in the spices, fry them for 5 minutes.

Meanwhile, in a small bowl, beat the yogurt with the saffron and the salt.

Add the yogurt mixture to the cooker stirring well to blend. Bring to HIGH pressure and cook for 10 minutes.

Reduce the pressure with cold water.

Return the open cooker to moderate heat and stir in the lemon juice.

Sprinkle over the chopped coriander leaves and cook for 5 minutes.

Transfer the curry to a warmed serving dish. Garnish with the lemon slices and serve immediately.

LIVER PATE

about 700g (1½ lb)
30 minutes HIGH pressure

Metric/Imperial

1 teaspoon butter
500g (1lb) lamb's liver, finely chopped
125ml (4oz) lean beef, minced
3 anchovy fillets, chopped
3 garlic cloves, crushed
1 medium-sized onion, peeled and finely chopped
2 tablespoons chopped fresh parsley
75ml (3fl oz) brandy
2 tablespoons tomato purée
½ teaspoon salt
½ teaspoon black pepper
½ teaspoon dried sage
½ teaspoon grated nutmeg
6 tablespoons fine dry breadcrumbs
600ml (1 pint) hot water

American

1 teaspoon butter
1lb lamb's livers, finely chopped
¼lb lean beef, ground
3 anchovy fillets, chopped
3 garlic cloves, crushed
1 medium-sized onion, peeled and finely chopped
2 tablespoons chopped fresh parsley
⅓ cup brandy
2 tablespoons tomato purée
½ teaspoon salt
½ teaspoon black pepper
½ teaspoon dried sage
½ teaspoon grated nutmeg
6 tablespoons fine dry breadcrumbs
2½ cups hot water

Lightly grease a medium-sized terrine or heatproof dish with the butter. Set aside.

If you have an electric blender place the liver, beef, anchovies, garlic, onion, parsley, brandy and tomato purée in the container and blend until the mixture is smooth. Spoon the mixture into a large mixing bowl. Alternatively, mince [grind] together the liver, beef, anchovies, garlic, onion and parsley.

Add the brandy and tomato purée, beating well with a wooden spoon to blend.

Add the salt, pepper, sage, nutmeg and breadcrumbs, beating well with a wooden spoon.

Spoon the mixture into the prepared terrine or dish and cover with aluminium foil.

Pour the water into the cooker and place the terrine or dish on the trivet. Bring to HIGH pressure and cook for 30 minutes.

Allow the pressure to reduce at room temperature.

Remove the dish from the cooker and discard the aluminium foil. Set aside to cool completely. When the pâté is quite cool, place a heavy weight on top and leave for at least 6 hours before serving.

Serve the pâté straight from the terrine or turn it out. To turn it out, run a sharp knife around the edge of the pâté. Place a plate, inverted, on top and reverse the two. The pâté should slide out easily. Cut into thin slices and serve.

HAM BRAISED IN WHITE WINE

6 servings
36 minutes HIGH pressure
6 minutes HIGH pressure

Metric/Imperial

1 × 1.25kg (1 × 3lb) ham
50g (2oz) butter
1 tablespoon vegetable oil
1 medium-sized onion, peeled and thinly sliced
1 large carrot, scraped and sliced
400ml (15fl oz) warmed dry, white wine
bouquet garni, consisting of 4 parsley sprigs, 1 thyme spray and 1 bay leaf tied together
2 spring onions, thinly sliced
225g (8oz) mushrooms, wiped clean and thinly sliced
¼ teaspoon salt
¼ teaspoon pepper
1 tablespoon beurre manié, made by blending together 1 tablespoon butter with 2 tablespoons flour
150ml (5fl oz) double cream

American

1 x 3lb ham
4 tablespoons butter
1 tablespoon vegetable oil
1 medium-sized onion, peeled and thinly sliced
1 large carrot, scraped and sliced
2 cups warmed dry, white wine
bouquet garni, consisting of 4 parsley sprigs, 1 thyme spray and 1 bay leaf tied together
2 green onions, thinly sliced
½lb mushrooms, wiped clean and thinly sliced
¼ teaspoon salt
¼ teaspoon pepper
1 tablespoon beurre manié, made by blending together 1 tablespoon butter with 2 tablespoons flour
½ cup heavy cream

First pre-cook the ham. Remove the trivet and place the ham in the cooker. Pour over enough water to cover. Bring to the boil in the open cooker over moderate heat. Remove the cooker from the heat. Remove the ham and pour away the water. Return the ham to the cooker. Pour over enough fresh water to cover but do not fill the cooker more than half full. Bring to HIGH pressure and cook for 36 minutes.

Allow the pressure to reduce at room temperature.

Remove the ham from the cooker, using two large forks. With a sharp knife, remove and discard the skin and excess fat. Wrap the ham in aluminium foil and keep warm. Discard the cooking liquid.

Rinse out the cooker. Melt 25g (1oz) [2 tablespoons] of the butter with the oil in the open cooker over moderate heat. When the foam subsides, add the onion and carrot and fry, stirring occasionally, for 5 to 7 minutes, or until the onion is soft and translucent but not brown.

Pour in the wine and add the bouquet garni. Bring to the boil in the open cooker over moderate heat, and cook for 2 minutes.

Remove the foil from the ham. Using large forks, transfer the ham to the cooker. Bring to HIGH pressure and cook for 6 minutes.

Allow the pressure to reduce at room temperature.

Using 2 large forks, transfer the ham to a plate. Wrap it in aluminium foil and keep warm, while you prepare the sauce.

In a medium-sized frying-pan, melt

the remaining butter over moderate heat. When the foam subsides, add the spring onions and cook, stirring occasionally, for 2 to 3 minutes or until they are soft. Add the mushrooms and cook, stirring occasionally, for 3 to 4 minutes, or until they are very lightly browned. Sprinkle over the salt and pepper.

Remove the pan from the heat. Set aside.

Pour the cooking liquid from the pressure cooker through a strainer placed over a medium-sized mixing bowl. Discard the contents of the strainer. Return the liquid to the open cooker and place over high heat. Boil the liquid rapidly for 5 minutes or until it has reduced by about half.

Reduce the heat to low and add the beurre manié, a little at a time, stirring constantly. Continue cooking, stirring constantly, for a further 2 to 3 minutes, or until the sauce is thick and smooth.

Add the mushroom mixture to the sauce and stir in the cream. Continue cooking for a further 2 minutes or until the sauce is heated through but not boiling. Taste the sauce and add more salt if necessary.

Remove the cooker from the heat and pour the sauce into a warmed sauceboat Set aside and keep warm.

Carve the ham into slices and arrange them on a warmed serving plate. Pour over a little of the sauce and serve the remainder separately. Serve immediately.

OXTAIL CASSEROLE

4 servings
40 minutes HIGH pressure
5 minutes HIGH pressure

Metric/Imperial

2 tablespoons vegetable oil
1.5kg (3lb) prepared oxtail pieces
2 medium-sized onions, peeled and
　　sliced
2 large carrots, scraped and sliced
4 medium-sized potatoes, peeled and
　　sliced
1 leek, washed, trimmed and cut into
　　thick slices
125g (4oz) mushrooms, wiped clean
　　and sliced
bouquet garni, consisting of 4 parsley
　　sprigs, 1 thyme spray and 1 bay leaf
　　tied together
½ teaspoon salt
¼ teaspoon black pepper
⅛ teaspoon celery salt
¼ teaspoon dried thyme
¼ teaspoon dried marjoram
½ teaspoon Worcestershire sauce
juice of ½ lemon
600ml (1 pint) hot beef stock
2 teaspoons tomato purée

American

2 tablespoons vegetable oil
3lb oxtail pieces
2 medium-sized onions, peeled and
　　sliced
2 large carrots, scraped and sliced
4 medium-sized potatoes, peeled and
　　sliced
1 leek, washed, trimmed and cut into
　　thick slices
¼lb mushrooms, wiped clean and sliced
bouquet garni, consisting of 4 parsley
　　sprigs, 1 thyme spray and 1 bay leaf
　　tied together
½ teaspoon salt
¼ teaspoon black pepper
⅛ teaspoon celery salt
¼ teaspoon dried thyme
¼ teaspoon dried marjoram
½ teaspoon Worcestershire sauce
juice of ½ lemon
2½ cups hot beef stock
2 teaspoons tomato purée

Remove the trivet. Heat the oil in the open cooker over moderate heat. When the oil is hot, add the oxtail pieces and cook them, turning occasionally, for 5 minutes, or until they are evenly browned. Using tongs or a large spoon, transfer them to a warmed plate and set aside.

Add the onions and carrots to the cooker and cook, stirring occasionally, for 8 to 10 minutes, or until the onions are golden brown.

Add the potatoes, leek, mushrooms, bouquet garni, salt, pepper, celery salt, thyme, marjoram, Worcestershire sauce, lemon juice, tomato purée and stock. Stir well. Return the oxtail to the cooker. Bring to HIGH pressure and cook for 40 minutes.

Allow the pressure to reduce at room temperature.

Remove and discard the bouquet garni. Set aside to cool completely. When the stew is cool, transfer it to

a large dish and place it in the refrigerator to chill for at least 8 hours.

Remove the dish from the refrigerator. Remove and discard the fat that has risen to the surface. Return the stew to the pressure cooker. Bring to HIGH pressure and cook for 5 minutes.

Allow the pressure to reduce at room temperature.

Transfer the casserole to a warmed serving dish and serve immediately.

SWEET AND SOUR BEEF

6 servings
40 minutes HIGH pressure

Metric/Imperial

1 × 1.25kg (1 × 3lb) top rump of beef
1 teaspoon salt
½ teaspoon black pepper
50ml (2fl oz) vegetable oil
2 large onions, peeled and thinly sliced
2 large carrots, scraped and thinly
　　sliced
400ml (15fl oz) warmed red wine
150ml (5fl oz) red wine vinegar
50g (2oz) sugar
bouquet garni, consisting of 4 parsley
　　sprigs, 1 thyme spray and 1 bay leaf
　　tied together
½ teaspoon finely grated lemon rind
125g (4oz) stoned prunes, chopped
1 tablespoon beurre manié made by
　　blending together 1 tablespoon
　　butter and 2 tablespoons flour
12 canned prunes, drained

American

1 x 3lb pot roast rump
1 teaspoon salt
½ teaspoon black pepper
¼ cup vegetable oil
2 large onions, peeled and thinly sliced
2 large carrots, scraped and thinly
　　sliced
2 cups warmed red wine
½ cup red wine vinegar
¼ cup sugar
bouquet garni, consisting of 4 parsley
　　sprigs, 1 thyme spray and 1 bay leaf
　　tied together
½ teaspoon finely grated lemon rind
¾ cup pitted chopped prunes
1 tablespoon beurre manié, made by
　　blending together 1 tablespoon
　　butter with 2 tablespoons flour
12 canned prunes, drained

Sweet and Sour Beef is an interesting variation on more traditional pot roasts.

Rub the meat all over with the salt and pepper and set aside.

Remove the trivet. Heat the oil in the open cooker over moderate heat. When the oil is hot, add the beef and, turning frequently, cook for 10 to 12 minutes, or until it is evenly browned on all sides. Remove the meat, using two large forks, and set aside.

Add the onions and the carrots and cook stirring occasionally for 5 to 7 minutes, or until the onions are soft and translucent but not brown.

Pour in the wine, vinegar, sugar, bouquet garni, lemon rind and the chopped prunes. Stir well to mix the ingredients thoroughly. Remove the cooker from the heat.

Insert the trivet. Place the beef on the trivet and return the cooker to the heat. Bring to HIGH pressure and cook for 40 minutes.

Reduce the pressure with cold water. Using two large forks, remove the meat from the cooker and transfer to a warmed plate. Cover with aluminium foil and set aside. Keep warm while you make the sauce.

Remove the trivet. With a metal spoon, skim off any fat from the cooking liquid. Pour the liquid through a strainer held over a large mixing bowl, pressing down on the vegetables and prunes with the back of a wooden spoon. Discard the contents of the strainer. Return the liquid to the cooker.

Boil the liquid in the open cooker over moderately high heat for 10-15 minutes or until it has reduced by about one-third. Reduce the heat to low and stir in the beurre manié, a little at a time, stirring constantly, until the sauce is thick and smooth. Remove the cooker from the heat and set aside.

Remove and discard the foil from the beef. Place the meat on a carving board. Carve it into thick slices and transfer the slices to a warmed serving dish.

Pour over the sauce and garnish with the whole prunes. Serve immediately.

ESSEX MEAT LAYER PUDDING

3-4 servings
20 minutes pre-steaming
1¼ hours LOW pressure

Metric/Imperial

SUET PASTRY
175g (6oz) flour
¼ teaspoon salt
75g (3oz) shredded suet
125ml (4fl oz) cold water
2 teaspoons butter
FILLING
25g (1oz) butter
2 medium-sized onions, peeled and finely chopped
225g (8oz) minced veal
225g (8oz) minced pork
1 teaspoon dried sage
¼ teaspoon dried oregano
¼ teaspoon black pepper
½ teaspoon salt
¼ teaspoon celery salt
1 tablespoon flour
1 tablespoon finely chopped chives
2 egg yolks

MEAT

2 tablespoons double cream
1½ litres (2½ pints) boiling water

American

SUET PASTRY
1 cup flour
¼ teaspoon salt
3oz shredded suet
½ cup cold water
2 teaspoons butter
FILLING
2 tablespoons butter
2 medium-sized onions, peeled and
   finely chopped
½lb ground veal
½lb ground pork
1 teaspoon dried sage

¼ teaspoon dried oregano
¼ teaspoon black pepper
½ teaspoon salt
¼ teaspoon celery salt
1 tablespoon flour
1 tablespoon finely chopped chives
2 egg yolks
2 tablespoons heavy cream
6 cups boiling water

To make the pastry, sift the flour and salt into a medium-sized mixing bowl.

Using your fingers, rub the suet into the flour mixture, until the ingredients are thoroughly combined. Add just enough water to make a stiff dough that will roll out easily. Form the dough into a ball and wrap it in greaseproof or waxed paper. Place the dough in the refrigerator to chill for 10 minutes.

To make the filling, in a large frying-pan, melt the butter over moderate heat. When the foam subsides, add the onions. Fry them, stirring occasionally, for 8 to 10 minutes, or until they are soft and golden.

Add the veal, pork, sage, oregano, pepper, salt, celery salt and flour to the pan. Stir well to mix and cook, stirring occasionally, for 5 minutes. Stir in the chives and remove the pan from the heat.

Made with pork, veal and suet pastry, Essex Layer Pudding is a warming dish from the east coast of England.

In a small mixing bowl, beat the egg yolks and the cream together with a fork. Stir the egg yolk and cream mixture into the meat mixture in the frying-pan. Return the pan to the heat and cook, stirring occasionally, for a further 5 minutes. Remove the pan from the heat and set aside.

Using 1 teaspoon of the butter, grease a 1.5 litre (2½ pint) pudding basin [1½ quart round casserole]. Take the pastry out of the refrigerator. Turn the dough out on to a lightly floured board. Using a floured rolling pin, roll out the dough to a circle about 0.5cm (¼in) thick. Using a sharp knife, cut out a small circle of dough just large enough to fit the bottom of the container. Place the circle on the bottom of the container and top it with a layer—about 3cm (1½in)— of the filling mixture. Cut out another circle of dough just large enough to fit the new level of the bowl. Continue layering the filling and dough until all the ingredients have been used, finishing with a layer of the dough. There should be three layers of meat.

The ingredients will not completely fill the container but the extra space is needed to allow the pudding to rise during steaming.

Cut a circle out of greaseproof or waxed paper about 10cm (4in) wider in diameter than the rim. Grease the paper with the remaining butter. Cut out a circle of aluminium foil the same size as the paper circle.

Put the greaseproof or waxed paper circle and foil circle together, the buttered side of the greaseproof or waxed paper away from the foil and, holding them together, make a 3cm (1in) pleat across the centre. Place the pleated paper and foil circles, foil upper-most, over the pudding. With a piece of string, securely tie the paper and foil circle around the rim of the basin, leaving a loop with which to lift the pudding out of the cooker when cooked.

Remove the trivet. Pour the boiling water into the pressure cooker. Replace the trivet. Place the pudding on the trivet. Close the pressure cooker, but do not fit the indicator weight. Pre-steam over low for 20 minutes. This means that the water simmers and steam escapes through the vent.

Position the indicator weight. Bring to LOW pressure and cook for 1¼ hours. Allow the pressure to reduce at room temperature.

Lift the pudding out of the cooker. Remove the foil and paper circles.

Place a large serving plate, inverted, on top of the pudding. Holding them firmly together, reverse them. The pudding should slide out easily. Serve immediately.

KIDNEY CASSEROLE

3-4 servings
7 minutes HIGH pressure

Metric/Imperial

4 tablespoons seasoned flour, made with 4 tablespoons flour, 1 teaspoon salt and 1 teaspoon black pepper
12 lambs' kidneys, cleaned, prepared and sliced
50g (2oz) butter
8 streaky bacon slices, chopped
2 onions, peeled and sliced
2 garlic cloves, crushed
1 green pepper, white pith removed, seeded and sliced
2 tablespoons soy sauce
300ml (½ pint) hot beef stock
50ml (2fl oz) red wine
½ teaspoon dried basil

American

4 tablespoons seasoned flour, made with 4 tablespoons flour, 1 teaspoon salt and 1 teaspoon black pepper
12 lambs' kidneys, cleaned, prepared and sliced
4 tablespoons butter
8 bacon slices, chopped
2 onions, peeled and sliced
2 garlic cloves, crushed
1 green pepper, white membrane removed, seeded and sliced
2 tablespoons soy sauce
1¼ cups hot beef stock
¼ cup red wine
½ teaspoon dried basil

Sprinkle the seasoned flour on a plate. Roll the kidney slices in the flour mixture and coat them all over. Shake off any excess flour and set aside.

In the open cooker, melt the butter over moderate heat. When the foam subsides, add the bacon and fry it, stirring occasionally, for 5 minutes or until it is lightly browned. With a slotted spoon, transfer the bacon to a plate. Set aside for use later.

Add the onions, garlic and green pepper to the fat. Fry, stirring occasionally, for 5 to 7 minutes, or until the onions are soft and translucent but not brown. With a slotted spoon, transfer the vegetables to the plate with the bacon. Set aside.

Add the sliced kidneys to the cooker and cook, turning occasionally with a wooden spoon, for 3 minutes. Return the bacon and vegetables to the cooker. Pour over the soy sauce, the beef stock and the wine. Stir in the basil. Bring to HIGH pressure and cook for 7 minutes.

Allow the pressure to reduce at room temperature.

Transfer the kidney mixture to a warmed serving dish and serve immediately.

IRISH STEW

4 servings
15 minutes HIGH pressure

Metric/Imperial

12 lamb cutlets, from the scrag or middle neck
500g (1lb) onions, peeled and thickly sliced
1kg (2lb) potatoes, peeled and sliced
1 teaspoon salt
½ teaspoon black pepper
½ teaspoon dried marjoram
400ml (15fl oz) water

American

6 lamb shoulder chops
1lb onions, peeled and thickly sliced
2lb potatoes, peeled and sliced
1 teaspoon salt
½ teaspoon black pepper
½ teaspoon dried marjoram
2 cups water

Trim as much fat as possible from the meat.

Remove the trivet. Arrange a layer of meat on the bottom of the cooker. Cover with a layer of onion and then potato. Sprinkle with a little of the salt, pepper and marjoram. Continue making layers in this way, adding the seasoning, until all the ingredients are used up. Pour over the water. Bring to HIGH pressure and cook for 15 minutes.

Allow the pressure to reduce at room temperature.

Transfer the stew to a warmed serving dish and serve immediately.

GERMAN VEAL STEW WITH ASPARAGUS

6-8 servings
12 minutes HIGH pressure

Metric/Imperial

50g (2oz) butter
4 tablespoons vegetable oil
1kg (2lb) stewing or pie veal, cut into 3cm (1in) cubes
1 small onion, peeled and finely chopped
225g (8oz) mushrooms, wiped clean and thinly sliced
150ml (5fl oz) hot chicken stock
300ml (10fl oz) white wine
1 teaspoon dried thyme
1 teaspoon salt
½ teaspoon black pepper
25g (2oz) beurre manié, made by blending 2 tablespoons butter with 4 tablespoons flour
700g (1½lb) canned asparagus, drained and cut into 3cm (1in) pieces
125ml (4fl oz) single cream
grated rind of 1 lemon

American

4 tablespoons butter
4 tablespoons vegetable oil
2lb stewing veal, cut into 1in cubes
1 small onion, peeled and finely chopped
½lb mushrooms, wiped clean and thinly sliced
2/3 cup hot chicken stock
1¼ cups white wine
1 teaspoon dried thyme
1 teaspoon salt
½ teaspoon black pepper
2 tablespoons beurre manié, made by blending 2 tablespoons butter with 4 tablespoons flour
1½lb canned asparagus, drained and cut into 1in pieces
½ cup light cream
grated rind of 1 lemon

Remove the trivet. Melt the butter with the oil in the open cooker over moderate heat. When the foam subsides, add the veal and onion. Fry, stirring occasion-ally, for 6 to 8 minutes, or until the veal is evenly browned.

Add the mushrooms and cook for 3 minutes, stirring frequently.

Pour in the stock and wine and add the thyme, salt and pepper. Bring to HIGH pressure and cook for 12 minutes.

Allow the pressure to reduce at room temperature.

Place the open cooker over low heat. Add the beurre manié, a little at a time, stirring constantly. Add the asparagus and the cream, stirring constantly. Continue to cook, stirring constantly, for a further 3 to 4 minutes, or until the asparagus is heated through.

Transfer the mixture to a warmed serving dish. Sprinkle over the grated lemon rind and serve immediately.

LAMB AND MUSHROOM STEW

4 servings
12 minutes HIGH pressure

Metric/Imperial

50g (2oz) seasoned flour, made with 50g (2oz) flour, 2 tablespoons dried rosemary, 1 teaspoon salt and ½ teaspoon black pepper
1kg (2lb) boned leg of lamb, cut into 5cm (2in) cubes
50g (2oz) butter
3 medium-sized onions, thinly sliced
500g (1lb) mushrooms, wiped clean and sliced
½ teaspoon salt
¼ teaspoon black pepper
300ml (10fl oz) hot chicken stock
225ml (8fl oz) sour cream

American

½ cup seasoned flour, made with ½ cup flour, 2 tablespoons dried rosemary, 1 teaspoon salt and ½ teaspoon black pepper
2lb boned leg of lamb, cut into 2in cubes
4 tablespoons butter
3 medium-sized onions, thinly sliced
1lb mushrooms, wiped clean and sliced
½ teaspoon salt
¼ teaspoon black pepper
1¼ cups hot chicken stock
1 cup sour cream

Place the seasoned flour on a shallow plate. Roll the meat cubes in it, shaking off any excess flour. Set the coated cubes aside.

Remove the trivet. Melt the butter in the open cooker over moderate heat. When the foam subsides, add the onions and cook, stirring occasionally for 5 to 7 minutes, or until the onions are soft and translucent but not brown. Add the lamb cubes and, stirring and turning occasionally, cook for 5 minutes, or until the meat is evenly and lightly brown.

Add the mushrooms, salt, pepper and hot chicken stock and mix well to blend. Bring to HIGH pressure and cook for 12 minutes.

Reduce the pressure with cold water.

Return the open cooker to heat. Stir in the sour cream and mix well to blend. Heat the mixture gently over low heat until it is hot but not boiling.

Transfer the stew to a warmed serving dish and serve immediately.

STEAMED MEAT LOAF

4 servings
45 minutes LOW pressure

Metric/Imperial

700g (1½lb) lean pork, minced
400g (14oz) canned, peeled tomatoes, drained
125g (4oz) frozen green beans, thawed and drained
175g (6oz) small macaroni, cooked and drained
1 garlic clove, crushed
1 teaspoon salt
1 teaspoon black pepper
2 tablespoons tomato purée
½ teaspoon dried thyme
1 egg, lightly beaten
2 teaspoons butter
1½ litres (2½ pints) boiling water

American

1½lb lean pork, ground
14oz can peeled tomatoes, drained
1½ cups frozen green beans, thawed and drained
1½ cups small macaroni, cooked and drained
1 garlic clove, crushed
1 teaspoon salt
1 teaspoon black pepper

POT ROAST with BREWER'S GRAVY

6 servings
45 minutes HIGH pressure

Metric/Imperial

1 × 1.75kg (1 × 3lb) top rump of beef
1 teaspoon salt
½ teaspoon black pepper
50ml (2fl oz) vegetable oil
4 medium-sized leeks, cleaned and
    thinly sliced
6 medium-sized parsnips, peeled and
    sliced
900ml (1½ pints) hot beef stock
bouquet garni, consisting of
    4 parsley sprigs, 1 thyme spray and
    1 bay leaf tied together
225ml (8fl oz) light ale
1 tablespoon beurre manié, made by
    blending 1 tablespoon butter with
    2 tablespoons flour
4 parsley sprigs

American

1 x 3lb pot roast rump
1 teaspoon salt
½ teaspoon black pepper
4 tablespoons vegetable oil
4 medium-sized leeks, cleaned and
    thinly sliced
6 medium-sized parsnips, peeled and
    sliced
3¾ cups hot beef stock
bouquet garni, consisting of 4 parsley
    sprigs, 1 thyme spray and 1 bay leaf
    tied together
1 cup beer
1 tablespoon beurre manié, made by
    blending 1 tablespoon butter with
    2 tablespoons flour
4 parsley sprigs

2 tablespoons tomato purée
½ teaspoon dried thyme
1 egg, lightly beaten
2 teaspoons butter
6 cups boiling water

In a large mixing bowl, combine all the ingredients, except the butter and the boiling water, beating well to blend.

Using 1 teaspoon of the butter, lightly grease a 1.5 litre (2 pint) pudding basin [1½ quart round casserole]. Spoon the mixture into it—the mixture will not completely fill it, but will rise slightly during cooking.

Cut a circle of greaseproof or waxed paper about 10cm (4in) wider in diameter than the rim of the container. Grease the paper with the remaining butter. Cut out a circle of aluminium foil the same size as the paper circle.

Put the two circles together, with the buttered side of the greaseproof or waxed paper away from the foil.

This interesting steamed meat loaf only needs a salad accompaniment as it actually contains macaroni, as well as pork, tomatoes and green beans. It should be served hot straight from the cooker, with lots of lager to drink.

Holding them firmly together, make a 3cm (1in) pleat across the centre. Place the pleated paper and foil circle, foil uppermost, over the container. With a piece of string, securely tie the paper and foil circle around the rim.

Remove the trivet from the cooker. Pour in the boiling water and replace the trivet. Place the loaf on the trivet. Bring to LOW pressure and cook for 45 minutes.

Allow the pressure to reduce at room temperature.

Lift the loaf from the cooker. Remove and discard the foil and paper circles. Turn the loaf out on to a warmed serving dish. Serve immediately.

Rub the meat all over with the salt and pepper. Set aside.

Remove the trivet. Heat the vegetable oil in the open cooker over moderate heat. Add the beef and, turning frequently, cook for 10 to 12 minutes, or until it is evenly browned on all sides. Using two large forks, transfer the beef to a plate. Put half of the sliced leeks and half of the parsnips into the cooker and fry, stirring occasionally for 8 minutes.

Add the bouquet garni. Replace the trivet and put the beef on it. Pour over the hot beef stock. Bring to HIGH pressure and cook for 45 minutes.

Allow the pressure to reduce at room temperature.

Transfer the beef to a plate. Cover with aluminium foil and keep warm.

Using a large fork, remove the trivet. With a metal spoon, skim off any fat from the liquid in the cooker. Strain the cooking liquid into a large bowl. Discard the contents of the strainer.

Return the liquid to the open cooker and add the remaining vegetables. Boil the liquid rapidly over moderately high heat for 20 minutes or until it has reduced by about half.

Stir in the beer and bring the sauce to the boil again. Reduce the heat to low and add the beurre manié, a little at a time, stirring constantly until the gravy is rich and smooth. Remove from the heat and keep warm.

Remove and discard the foil from the beef. Carve the beef into thick slices and arrange them on a warmed serving plate. Pour over the gravy and vegetables. Garnish with the parsley sprigs and serve immediately.

Pot Roast with Brewer's gravy uses beer for flavour, as the name implies.

BEEF CASSEROLE

4 servings
20 minutes HIGH pressure

Metric/Imperial

25g (1oz) seasoned flour, made with 25g (1oz) flour, 1 teaspoon salt, ½ teaspoon black pepper
700g (1½lb) stewing steak, cut into cubes
25g (1oz) butter
1 tablespoon vegetable oil
2 medium-sized onions, peeled and sliced
4 carrots, scraped and sliced
125g (4oz) mushrooms, wiped clean and sliced
600ml (1 pint) hot beef stock
1 tablespoon beurre manié made by blending 1 tablespoon butter with 2 tablespoons flour

American

¼ cup seasoned flour, made with ¼ cup flour, 1 teaspoon salt and ½ teaspoon black pepper
1½lb stewing beef, cut into cubes
2 tablespoons butter
1 tablespoon vegetable oil
2 medium-sized onions, peeled and sliced
4 carrots, scraped and sliced
¼lb mushrooms, wiped clean and sliced
2½ cups hot beef stock
1 tablespoon beurre manié, made by blending 1 tablespoon butter with 2 tablespoons flour

Put the seasoned flour on a plate. Toss the meat cubes in the flour to coat them. Shake off any excess flour.

Remove the trivet. Melt the butter with the oil over moderate heat. Add the meat, onions and carrots and cook, stirring occasionally, for 7 minutes, or until the meat is browned on all sides. Add the mushrooms and cook for a further 2 minutes, stirring occasionally.

Pour over the beef stock and bring to HIGH pressure. Cook for 20 minutes.

Allow the pressure to reduce at room temperature.

Return the open cooker to moderate heat. Add the beurre manié, a little at a time, stirring constantly until the sauce is thick.

Transfer the casserole to a warmed serving dish and serve immediately.

BLANQUETTE DE VEAU

4 servings
12 minutes HIGH pressure

Metric/Imperial

700g (1½lb) veal, shoulder or breast,
    cut into cubes
600ml (1 pint) water
2 medium-sized onions, peeled and
    studded with 2 cloves each
2 medium-sized carrots, scraped and
    cut into quarters
300ml (10fl oz) white wine
bouquet garni, consisting of
    4 parsley sprigs, 1 thyme spray
    and 1 bay leaf tied
    together
½ teaspoon salt
⅛ teaspoon white pepper
1 tablespoon butter
2 tablespoons flour
50ml (2fl oz) single cream
2 egg yolks
4 slices white bread, toasted and cut
    into triangles

American

1½lb veal, shoulder or breast, cut into
    cubes
2½ cups water

*Veal in a creamy white wine sauce,
Blanquette de Veau is garnished with
lightly toasted triangles.*

2 medium-sized onions, peeled and
    studded with 2 cloves each
2 medium-sized carrots, scraped and
    cut into quarters
1¼ cups white wine
bouquet garni, consisting of 4 parsley
    sprigs, 1 thyme spray and 1 bay leaf
    tied together
½ teaspoon salt
⅛ teaspoon white pepper
1 tablespoon butter
2 tablespoons flour
¼ cup light cream
2 egg yolks
4 slices white bread, toasted and cut
    into triangles

Remove the trivet. Put the veal into the
cooker and pour over the water. Bring
the water to the boil in the open cooker
over moderate heat. Using a metal
spoon skim off any scum that rises to
the surface.

Add the onions, carrots, wine, bouquet garni, salt and pepper. Bring to
HIGH pressure and cook for 12
minutes.

Allow the pressure to reduce at room

temperature.

Strain the cooking liquid into a large
mixing bowl and set aside.

Discard the onions, carrots and
bouquet garni. Transfer the veal to a
warmed serving dish. Keep warm while
you prepare the sauce.

Melt the butter in a medium-sized
saucepan over low heat. Stir in the
flour with a wooden spoon. Cook for
2 minutes, stirring constantly. Remove
the pan from the heat. Stirring constantly, gradually add 600ml (1 pint)
[2½ cups] of the reserved stock. Return
the pan to the heat and, stirring constantly, bring the sauce to the boil.
Continue stirring and boil for 3
minutes or until the sauce becomes
thick and smooth. Remove the pan from
the heat. Set aside.

In a small bowl, beat the cream and
egg yolks together with a wooden
spoon. Stir in the hot sauce, 4 table
spoons at a time, mixing well to blend.
Return the mixture to the pan, beating
well with a wire whisk. Return the pan
to low heat, and heat gently, stirring
constantly, until it is hot but not
boiling.

Pour the sauce over the veal. Arrange
the toast triangles around the dish to
garnish and serve immediately.

POULTRY & GAME

Poultry is so adaptable, you can make a huge variety of delicious and unusual meals. Why not adopt the French custom of pot roasting chicken with a selection of vegetables in the cooking liquid and then serve as two courses—first the liquid, thickened slightly after cooking, as a soup and then the chicken as a main course?

Pressure cooking preserves the taste and texture of poultry, which are often so easily lost in these days of concentrated farming. Even boiling fowls are speedily transformed into succulent and tasty dishes.

When game is in season it can make a delightful change to the menu. With a pressure cooker you can make adventurous experiments with no extra trouble.

General hints

If you are using frozen poultry, it must be allowed to thaw at room temperature for 24 hours. Do not forget to remove the giblets before cooking. Frozen chicken pieces must also be thawed.

Prepare the fowl in the usual way. Rinse out the body cavity and dry with kitchen paper towels. If you are coating it with a sauce, skin the chicken before cooking.

If you are stuffing a chicken, calculate the cooking time on the stuffed weight. Chickens up to 1.5kg (3½lb), weighed after stuffing, are recommended for the best results. The bird should fit comfortably on the trivet and allow plenty of room for steam to circulate with no danger of the vent becoming blocked.

Various liquids can be used for cooking poultry. Wine and stock are the most popular and perhaps achieve the most delicious results. Allow a minimum of 300ml (10fl oz) [1¼ cups].

Remove the trivet and melt 25g (1oz) [2 tablespoons] butter with 1 tablespoon of vegetable oil over moderate heat. When the foam subsides, add the bird and cook for 10 minutes, turning with 2 large forks, until it is brown on all sides. Remove the bird and pour off any surplus fat.

Add the liquid to the cooker. Do not add cold liquid as too much can be lost through evaporation. Stock should be hot and the wine can then be stirred in without any loss through steam. If you are using wine alone, warm it first.

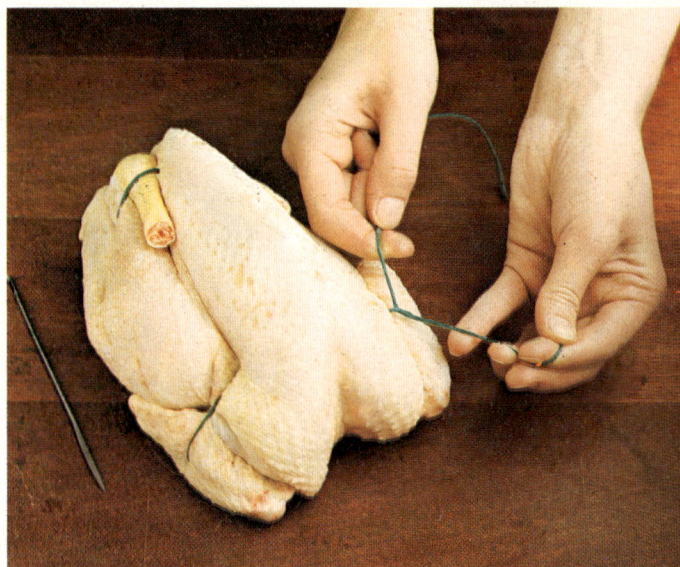

The giblets can be added to give extra flavour and chicken responds well to many herbs, particularly tarragon and basil. Replace the trivet and position the chicken centrally on it. Cook at HIGH pressure for the required time and after cooking reduce the pressure with cold water.

Use the cooking liquid to make gravy or a sauce to accompany the chicken or strain and reserve as stock for use later.

Above : It is often worth buying an untrussed fowl, whether game or poultry, and trussing it yourself. Pressure cookers are perfect for pot roasting or boiling, and make delicious stock. Even an apparently tough boiling fowl (right) can be delicious stuffed with a herb and onion mixture and steamed with carrots, celery and parsnips. And you can save the cooking liquid to use as the basis for a delicious chicken broth or as stock for use in innumerable other recipes.

Cooking times (HIGH pressure)

Chicken	poussin, halved	5-7 minutes	**Hare**	jointed [pieces]	35-40 minutes
	roasting, whole	5 minutes per 500g (1lb)	**Partridge**	whole	7-10 minutes
				jointed [pieces]	5- 7 minutes
	jointed [pieces]	5-7 minutes	**Pheasant**	whole	7-10 minutes
	boiling, whole	10 minutes per 500g (1lb)		jointed [pieces]	5- 7 minutes
	jointed [pieces]	15 minutes	**Rabbit**	jointed [pieces]	12-15 minutes
Frozen pieces	thawed	5-7 minutes	**Venison**		15 minutes per 500g (1lb)
Duck	whole	12-15 minutes per 500g (1lb)			
	jointed [pieces]	12 minutes			

CHICKEN AND PEAR CASEROLE

4 servings
12 minutes HIGH pressure

Metric/Imperial

1 × 1.25kg (1 × 3lb) chicken, cut into
   pieces
½ teaspoon salt
¼ teaspoon black pepper
½ teaspoon grated nutmeg
¼ teaspoon ground mace
50g (2oz) butter
2 onions, peeled and finely chopped
500g (1lb) conference pears, peeled,
   cored and quartered
300ml (10fl oz) warmed dry white wine
150ml (5fl oz) sour cream
2 teaspoons cornflour dissolved in
   2 tablespoons dry white wine

American

1 x 3lb chicken, cut into pieces
½ teaspoon salt
¼ teaspoon black pepper
½ teaspoon grated nutmeg
¼ teaspoon ground mace
4 tablespoons butter
2 onions, peeled and finely chopped
1lb firm pears, peeled, cored and
   quartered
1¼ cups warmed dry white wine
½ cup sour cream
2 teaspoons cornstarch dissolved in
   2 tablespoons dry white wine

Place the chicken pieces on a working surface. Using your fingertips, rub them all over with the salt, pepper, nutmeg and mace. Set aside.

Remove the trivet. Melt the butter in the open cooker over moderate heat. When the foam subsides, add the onions and fry, stirring occasionally, for 5 to 7 minutes, or until the onions are soft but not brown. Add the chicken pieces and fry, turning them occasionally, for 6 to 8 minutes or until they are lightly browned all over. Add the pears and pour over the wine. Bring to HIGH pressure and cook for 12 minutes.

Reduce the pressure with cold water.

Using a slotted spoon, transfer the chicken pieces and pear slices to a warmed serving dish. Set aside and keep warm while you finish off the sauce.

Place the open cooker over low heat.

Stir in the sour cream. Add the cornflour [cornstarch] mixture, stirring constantly, and cook for 3 to 4 minutes, or until the sauce is smooth and fairly thick.

Pour the sauce over the chicken and pears and serve immediately.

CHICKEN BREASTS with TARRAGON

6 servings
7 minutes HIGH pressure

Metric/Imperial

6 chicken breasts, skinned and boned
2 tablespoons seasoned flour, made
   with 2 tablespoons flour, ½ teaspoon
   salt and ½ teaspoon black pepper
50g (2oz) butter
2 shallots or spring onions, finely
   chopped
150ml (5fl oz) hot chicken stock
150ml (5fl oz) dry white wine
1 teaspoon dried tarragon
50ml (2fl oz) double cream

American

6 chicken breasts, skinned and boned
2 tablespoons seasoned flour, made
   with 2 tablespoons flour, ½ teaspoon
   salt and ½ teaspoon black pepper
4 tablespoons butter
2 shallots or green onions, finely
   chopped
⅔ cup hot chicken stock
⅔ cup dry white wine
1 teaspoon dried tarragon
¼ cup heavy cream

Coat the chicken breasts thoroughly with the seasoned flour. Set aside.

Remove the trivet. Melt half the butter in the open cooker over moderate heat. When the foam subsides, add the chicken breasts and brown them for 5 to 7 minutes on both sides. Using tongs, transfer the chicken breasts to a plate. Set aside.

Add the shallot or spring [green] onions to the cooker and fry them, stirring occasionally, for 4 to 5 minutes.

Return the chicken pieces to the cooker and pour over the stock and the wine. Add the tarragon. Bring to HIGH pressure and cook for 7 minutes.

Reduce the pressure with cold water.

Using tongs, transfer the chicken breasts to a warmed serving dish. Set aside and keep warm while you finish off the sauce.

Boil the cooking liquid rapidly in the open cooker over high heat for 5 minutes or until it has reduced by about half.

Reduce the heat to moderately low and stir in the remaining butter and the cream. Continue cooking, stirring constantly for 2 to 3 minutes or until it is thick and smooth.

Pour the sauce over the chicken breasts and serve immediately.

COQ AU VIN

4 servings
7 minutes HIGH pressure
6 minutes HIGH pressure

Metric/Imperial

125g (4oz) butter
1.25g (3lb) chicken pieces
½ teaspoon salt
⅛ teaspoon black pepper
60ml (2fl oz) brandy
300ml (10fl oz) hot chicken stock
400ml (15fl oz) full-bodied dry red
   wine
1 tablespoon tomato purée
2 garlic cloves, crushed
bouquet garni, consisting of 4 parsley
   sprigs, 1 thyme spray and 1 bay leaf
   tied together
1 tablespoon oil
18 small onions, peeled and left whole
225g (8oz) mushrooms, wiped clean
   and sliced
1 tablespoon beurre manié, made by
   blending 1 tablespoon butter with
   2 tablespoons flour
2 tablespoons chopped fresh parsley

American

1 stick butter
3lb chicken pieces
½ teaspoon salt
⅛ teaspoon black pepper
¼ cup brandy
1¼ cups hot chicken stock
3¾ cups full-bodied dry
   red wine
1 tablespoon tomato purée
2 garlic cloves, crushed
bouquet garni, consisting of 4 parsley
   sprigs, 1 thyme spray and 1 bay leaf
   tied together

Reduce the pressure with cold water.

Meanwhile, melt 25g (1oz) [2 tablespoons] of the remaining butter with the oil in a large frying-pan over moderate heat. When the foam subsides, add the onions and, stirring occasionally, cook for 8 to 10 minutes, or until the onions are evenly browned.

With a slotted spoon, transfer the onions to the chicken mixture. Return the cooker to the heat and bring to HIGH pressure. Cook for 6 minutes.

Reduce the pressure with cold water.

Using a slotted spoon, transfer the chicken pieces and the onions to a warmed dish. Cover with aluminium foil. Set aside and keep warm while you finish off the sauce.

Remove and discard the bouquet garni. Simmer the cooking liquid in the open cooker over moderate heat for 2 minutes, skimming off any fat from the surface with a metal spoon. Increase the heat to high and boil the liquid rapidly until it has reduced by about half.

Meanwhile, melt the remaining butter in a medium-sized frying pan over moderate heat. When the foam subsides, add the mushrooms and cook, stirring occasionally, for 3 to 4 minutes. Set aside.

When the sauce in the open cooker has reduced, reduce the heat to low and add the beurre manié, a little at a time, stirring constantly. Continue cooking, stirring constantly, for 2 to 3 minutes or until the sauce is thick and smooth.

Add the reserved chicken pieces and the onions to the sauce. Stir in the mushrooms. Simmer for 5 minutes or until the chicken is heated through. Sprinkle over the parsley and serve immediately.

DHANSAK

6 servings
15 minutes HIGH pressure
10 minutes HIGH pressure

Metric/Imperial

125g (4oz) tur dhal (lentils)
25g (1oz) channa dhal (lentils)
50g (2oz) masoor dhal (lentils)
25g (1oz) moong dhal (lentils)
600ml (1 pint) water
½ teaspoon salt
3 tablespoons ghee (clarified butter) or vegetable oil

Above : Classic Coq au Vin is always a successful dinner party dish.

1 tablespoon oil
18 small onions, peeled and left whole
½lb mushrooms, wiped clean and sliced
1 tablespoon beurre manié, made by blending 1 tablespoon butter with 2 tablespoons flour
2 tablespoons chopped fresh parsley

Remove the trivet. Melt 50g (2oz) [4 tablespoons] of the butter in the open cooker over moderate heat. When the foam subsides, add the chicken pieces and cook them for 5 to 7 minutes on each side, or until they are lightly and evenly browned. Sprinkle over the salt and pepper and reduce the heat to low. Pour over the brandy and ignite it with a match. Shake the cooker gently until the flames die down.

Add the hot stock and the wine. Stir in the tomato purée, garlic and bouquet garni. Bring to HIGH pressure and cook for 7 minutes.

Dhansak is a deliciously spicy chicken and lentil dish, welcomed even by people who don't usually like curry!

3cm (1in) piece fresh root ginger, peeled and finely chopped
1 garlic clove, finely chopped
8 chicken pieces
½ tablespoon coarsely chopped mint
225g (8oz) aubergines, cut into cubes
225g (8oz) pumpkin, peeled and cut into cubes
125g (4oz) spinach, chopped
1 large onion, peeled and sliced
500g (1lb) tomatoes, blanched, peeled and chopped or 400g (14oz) canned, peeled tomatoes, drained
MASALA
4 tablespoons ghee (clarified butter) or vegetable oil
1 large onion, sliced
4cm (1½in) piece fresh root ginger, peeled and finely chopped
2 green chillis, seeded and finely chopped
3 garlic cloves, crushed
½ teaspoon ground cinnamon
½ teaspoon ground cardamom
½ teaspoon ground cloves
1½ teaspoon turmeric
1 teaspoon ground coriander
½ teaspoon chilli powder
3 tablespoons chopped coriander leaves

American

---

1 cup lentils
2½ cups water
½ teaspoon salt
3 tablespoons ghee (clarified butter) or vegetable oil
1in piece fresh root ginger, peeled and finely chopped
1 garlic clove, finely chopped
8 chicken pieces
½ tablespoon coarsely chopped mint
½lb eggplant, cut into cubes
½lb pumpkin, peeled and cut into cubes
4oz (2 cups) chopped spinach
1 large onion, peeled and sliced
1lb tomatoes, blanched, peeled and chopped or 14oz can peeled tomatoes, drained
MASALA
4 tablespoons ghee (clarified butter) or vegetable oil
1 large onion, sliced
1½in piece fresh root ginger, peeled and finely chopped
2 green chilis, seeded and finely chopped

3 garlic cloves, crushed
½ teaspoon ground cinnamon
½ teaspoon ground cardamom
½ teaspoon ground cloves
1½ teaspoons turmeric
1 teaspoon ground coriander
½ teaspoon chili powder
3 tablespoons chopped coriander leaves

Wash all the lentils thoroughly in cold running water and soak them for 10 minutes.

Remove the trivet. Drain the lentils and transfer them to the cooker. Pour over the water and add the salt. Bring the liquid to the boil in the open cooker. Bring to HIGH pressure and cook for 15 minutes.

Allow the pressure to reduce at room temperature.

Meanwhile, in a large frying-pan, heat the ghee or oil over high heat. When the oil is hot, reduce the heat to moderately low and add the ginger and garlic. Fry, stirring constantly, for 2 minutes. Add the chicken pieces and fry them, turning frequently, until they are golden brown on all sides.

Add the contents of the frying-pan to the lentils in the cooker. Stir in the mint, aubergines [eggplant], pumpkin, spinach, onion and tomatoes. Bring to HIGH pressure and cook for 10 minutes.

Reduce the pressure with cold water.

Meanwhile, prepare the masala. Heat the ghee or vegetable oil in a large saucepan over high heat. When the oil is hot, add the onion. Reduce the heat to moderate and fry, stirring frequently, for 8 to 10 minutes, or until it is golden brown. Add the ginger, chillis and garlic and continue cooking for 3 minutes. Add all the remaining ingredients except the coriander leaves, and, stirring constantly, fry them for 8 minutes. If the spices get too dry or if they show signs of burning, reduce the heat to low and sprinkle a little water in the pan. Set aside.

Remove the chicken pieces from the cooker and set aside.

Pour the vegetables and lentils into the masala and stir well. Return the pan to moderately high heat and, when the mixture comes to the boil, cover the pan, reduce the heat to low and simmer for 5 minutes. Taste the mixture and add more salt, if necessary.

Add the chicken pieces and continue cooking for a further 10 minutes.

Turn the dhansak into a warmed serving dish. Sprinkle over the chopped coriander leaves and serve immediately.

DUCK AND GRAPE CASSEROLE

4 servings
12 minutes per 500g (1lb)
HIGH pressure

Metric/Imperial

¼ teaspoon black pepper
½ teaspoon salt
¼ teaspoon dried thyme
⅛ teaspoon grated nutmeg
1 duck, trimmed of all skin and fat
2 tablespoons vegetable oil
400ml (15fl oz) warmed dry white wine
1 tablespoon blackcurrant jelly
1 bay leaf
1 tablespoon cornflour dissolved in 2 tablespoons water
225g (8oz) seeded black grapes

American

¼ teaspoon black pepper
½ teaspoon salt
¼ teaspoon dried thyme
⅛ teaspoon grated nutmeg
1 duck, trimmed of all skin and fat
2 tablespoons vegetable oil
2 cups warmed dry white wine
1 tablespoon grape jelly
1 bay leaf
1 tablespoon cornstarch dissolved in 2 tablespoons water
½lb seeded black grapes

In a small bowl, mix the black pepper, salt, thyme and nutmeg together. Rub the mixture over the duck and set it aside.

Remove the trivet. Heat the oil in the open cooker over moderate heat. Put the duck in the cooker and brown it well on all sides, turning it with two large spoons.

Add the wine, blackcurrant [grape] jelly and bay leaf and bring to HIGH presure. Cook for the required time.

Reduce the pressure with cold water.

Using two large spoons, transfer the duck to a carving board. Carve it into serving pieces. Transfer the duck to a large, warmed serving plate. Set aside and keep hot while you finish the sauce.

Stir the cornflour [cornstarch] mixture into the cooking liquid in the open cooker over moderate heat. Add the grapes and cook the sauce, stirring constantly, over moderate heat, for 5 to 7 minutes, or until the sauce is thick and smooth. Remove and discard the bay leaf.

Pour the sauce over the duck and serve immediately.

DUCK, SPANISH STYLE

4 servings
15 minutes HIGH pressure
12 minutes per 500g (1lb)
HIGH pressure

Metric/Imperial

SAUCE ESPAGNOLE
25g (1oz) butter
1 medium-sized onion, peeled and chopped
1 medium-sized carrot, scraped and chopped
4 large mushrooms, wiped clean and sliced
150ml (5fl oz) hot beef stock
150ml (5fl oz) white wine
bouquet garni, consisting of 4 parsley sprigs, 1 thyme spray and 1 bay leaf tied together
½ teaspoon salt
¼ teaspoon black pepper
2 cloves
DUCK
1 duck
1 tablespoon chopped fresh parsley
25g (1 oz) butter
½ teaspoon salt
¼ teaspoon black pepper
2 teaspoons grated orange rind
1 duck liver, washed, dried and finely chopped
300ml (10fl oz) beef stock
1 onion, peeled and sliced
1 onion, peeled, whole and studded with 4 cloves
3 parsley sprigs
1 thyme spray
1 bay leaf
5cm (2in) strip of lemon rind
1 tablespoon white wine vinegar
125g (4oz) stoned, black olives, blanched

American

SAUCE ESPAGNOLE
2 tablespoons butter
1 medium-sized onion, peeled and chopped
1 medium-sized carrot, scraped and chopped
4 large mushrooms, wiped clean and sliced
⅔ cup hot beef stock
⅔ cup white wine
bouquet garni, consisting of 4 parsley sprigs, 1 thyme spray and 1 bay leaf tied together
½ teaspoon salt
¼ teaspoon black pepper
2 cloves
DUCK
1 duck
1 tablespoon chopped fresh parsley
2 tablespoons butter
½ teaspoon salt
¼ teaspoon black pepper
2 teaspoons grated orange rind
1 duck liver, washed, dried and finely chopped
1¼ cups beef stock
1 onion, peeled and sliced
1 onion, peeled, whole and studded with 4 cloves
3 parsley sprigs
1 thyme spray
1 bay leaf

2in strip of lemon rind
1 tablespoon white wine vinegar
¾ cup pitted, black olives, blanched

First make the sauce espagnole. Melt the butter in the open cooker over moderate heat. When the foam subsides, add the onion and carrot and fry, stirring occasionally, for 8 to 10 minutes, or until the onion is golden brown. Add the mushrooms and cook, stirring frequently, for 2 minutes. Pour over the beef stock and the wine and add the bouquet garni, salt, pepper and cloves. Bring to HIGH pressure and cook for 15 minutes.

Allow the pressure to reduce at room temperature.

Pour the sauce through a strainer over a medium-sized mixing bowl, pressing down on the vegetables with the back of a wooden spoon. Discard the contents of the strainer. Reserve the sauce.

Rinse the cooker.

Prepare the duck for cooking by clipping the wing ends and trussing it so that the wings and legs are close to the body. Prick the skin around the thighs, back and lower breast.

In a small bowl, combine the parsley, butter, ¼ teaspoon salt, the pepper and orange rind. Add the liver to the mixture and blend well. Stuff the duck with the liver mixture and close the cavity with a trussing needle and string or a skewer. Weigh the duck after stuffing to give the cooking time.

Remove the trivet from the cooker. Pour in the stock and add the sliced and whole onions, parsley, thyme, bay leaf, lemon rind and the remaining salt. Replace the trivet and arrange the duck on it. Bring to HIGH pressure and cook for the required time.

Reduce the pressure with cold water.

Using two large spoons, transfer the duck to a warmed serving dish. Untruss the duck. Set aside and keep hot while you finish off the sauce.

Strain the cooking liquid into a medium-sized saucepan, pressing down on the vegetables with the back of a wooden spoon. Discard the contents of the strainer. Using a metal spoon, skim off any fat remaining on the surface of the liquid.

Add the reserved sauce espagnole, stirring well to mix. Place the pan over moderate heat and bring sauce to the boil. Stir in the vinegar and the olives and continue to cook for a further 2 to 3 minutes.

Pour the sauce over and around the duck. Serve immediately.

PARTRIDGE POT ROAST

4-6 servings
25 minutes HIGH pressure

Metric/Imperial

50g (2oz) butter
2 medium-sized onions, peeled and chopped
2 medium-sized carrots, scraped and sliced
6 slices streaky bacon, rinds removed and chopped
125g (4oz) mushrooms, wiped clean and sliced
4 partridges, trussed and larded
½ teaspoon salt
½ teaspoon black pepper
bouquet garni, consisting of 4 parsley sprigs, 1 thyme spray and 1 bay leaf tied together
600ml (1 pint) hot beef stock
125ml (4fl oz) red wine
1 tablespoon beurre manié, made by blending 1 tablespoon butter with 2 tablespoons flour
2 tablespoons chopped fresh parsley

American

4 tablespoons butter
2 medium-sized onions, peeled and chopped
2 medium-sized carrots, scraped and sliced
6 slices bacon, rinds removed and chopped
¼lb mushrooms, wiped clean and sliced
4 partridges, trussed and larded
½ teaspoon salt
½ teaspoon black pepper
bouquet garni, consisting of 4 parsley sprigs, 1 thyme spray and 1 bay leaf tied together
2½ cups hot beef stock
½ cup red wine
1 tablespoon beurre manié, made by blending 1 tablespoon butter with 2 tablespoons flour
2 tablespoons chopped fresh parsley

Remove the trivet from the cooker. Melt the butter in the open cooker over moderate heat. When the foam subsides, add the onions and carrots and fry, stirring occasionally, for 5 to 7 minutes or until the onions are soft and translucent but not brown.

Using a slotted spoon, transfer the vegetables to a warmed plate. Set aside.

Add the bacon and mushrooms to the cooker. Fry, stirring frequently, for 5 minutes, or until the bacon is crisp and has rendered most of its fat. With a slotted spoon, transfer the bacon mixture to the plate with the vegetables. Set aside.

Place the partridges in the cooker. Cook them, turning occasionally, for 6 to 8 minutes or until they are lightly and evenly browned.

Return the vegetables and bacon mixture to the cooker. Add the salt, pepper and bouquet garni. Pour over the stock and wine. Bring to HIGH pressure and cook for 25 minutes.

Reduce the pressure with cold water.

Using two large spoons or tongs, remove the partridges. Cut them into 4 pieces. Set aside and keep warm. Strain the cooking liquid and reserve it. Set the vegetables aside and keep warm. Remove and discard the bouquet garni.

Return the strained cooking liquid to the cooker. Boil the liquid in the open cooker over high heat for 5 to 7 minutes or until it has reduced by one-third.

Reduce the heat to low. Add the beurre manié, a little at a time, stirring constantly, for a further 2 minutes, or until the sauce is thick and smooth.

Replace the vegetables and the partridges in the cooker and stir in the parsley. Cook for a further 2 to 3 minutes or until the pot roast is heated through. Transfer to a warmed serving dish and serve immediately.

VENISON WITH SHERRY SAUCE

6 servings
45 minutes HIGH pressure

Metric/Imperial

1 × 1.25kg (1 × 3lb) haunch venison, boned and rolled
2 teaspoons salt
1 teaspoon black pepper
50ml (2fl oz) olive oil

5 slices streaky bacon, rinds removed
300ml (½ pint) hot beef stock
125g (4oz) bottled or canned cherries,
 drained, stoned and 50ml (2fl oz)
 cherry juice reserved
½ teaspoon coriander seeds, crushed
2 teaspoons white wine vinegar
50ml (2fl oz) dry sherry
1 tablespoon beurre manié, made by
 blending together 1 tablespoon
 butter with 2 tablespoons flour
MARINADE
300ml (½ pint) dry white wine
1 onion, peeled and chopped
1 garlic clove, finely chopped
1 celery stalk, trimmed and chopped
50ml (2fl oz) olive oil
1 marjoram sprig
2 teaspoons coriander seeds, crushed

American

1 x 3lb haunch venison, boned and
 rolled
2 teaspoons salt
1 teaspoon black pepper
¼ cup olive oil
5 slices bacon, rinds removed
1¼ cups hot beef stock
⅔ cup bottled or canned cherries
 drained, pitted and 4 tablespoons
 cherry juice reserved
½ teaspoon coriander seeds, crushed
2 teaspoons white wine vinegar
¼ cup dry sherry
1 tablespoon beurre manié, made by
 blending 1 tablespoon butter with
 2 tablespoons flour
MARINADE
1¼ cups dry white wine
1 onion, peeled and chopped
1 garlic clove, finely chopped
1 celery stalk, trimmed and chopped
¼ cup olive oil
1 marjoram sprig
2 teaspoons coriander seeds, crushed

First prepare the marinade. In a large, shallow dish, combine all of the marinade ingredients and stir well to blend. Add the venison to the dish and set aside to marinate at room temperature for 24 hours, basting occasionally.

Remove the venison from the marinade and pat it dry with kitchen paper towels. Pour the marinade through a fine wire strainer into a medium-sized mixing bowl and set aside. Discard the contents of the strainer.

Using your fingertips, rub the meat all over with the salt and pepper. Set aside.

Remove the trivet. Heat the oil in the open cooker over moderate heat. When the oil is hot, add the venison and cook, turning frequently, for 8 to 10 minutes, or until it is lightly browned all over.

Lay the bacon slices over the venison and pour the stock and reserved marinade into the cooker. Bring to HIGH pressure and cook for 45 minutes.

Reduce the pressure with cold water.

Using two large forks, transfer the venison to a carving board. Carve the venison into thick slices and arrange

A nourishing dish of partridges and vegetables, Partridge Pot Roast can be served with potatoes and peas.

them on a warmed serving plate. Keep hot while you make the sauce.

Boil the cooking liquid rapidly in the open cooker over high heat until it has reduced by about half. Reduce the heat to moderate and stir in the cherries, juice, coriander, vinegar and sherry. Cook, stirring frequently, for 5 minutes.

Add the beurre manié, a little at a time, stirring constantly until the sauce is thick and smooth.

Pour the sauce into a warmed sauceboat and serve with the venison.

HARE PUDDING

6 servings
20 minutes pre-steaming
1¼ hours LOW pressure

Metric/Imperial

2 tablespoons flour
1 small onion, peeled and thinly sliced
1 tablespoon redcurrant jelly
½ teaspoon salt
¼ teaspoon black pepper
1 teaspoon dried rosemary
1 teaspoon dried thyme
175ml (6fl oz) beef stock
50ml (2fl oz) dry red wine
800g (1½lb) hare meat, cut into small cubes
1.5 litres (2½ pints) boiling water
PASTRY
350g (12oz) flour
1 teaspoon baking powder
⅛ teaspoon salt
175g (6oz) shredded suet
200ml (7fl oz) water
1 teaspoon vegetable oil

American

2 tablespoons flour
1 small onion, peeled and thinly sliced
1 tablespoon redcurrant jelly
½ teaspoon salt
¼ teaspoon black pepper
1 teaspoon dried rosemary
1 teaspoon dried thyme
¾ cup beef stock
¼ cup dry red wine
1½lb hare meat, cut into small cubes
6 cups boiling water
PASTRY
2½ cups flour
1 teaspoon baking powder
⅛ teaspoon salt
6oz shredded suet
⅞ cup water
1 teaspoon vegetable oil

In a large, shallow mixing bowl, combine the flour, onion, redcurrant jelly, salt, pepper, rosemary, thyme, beef stock and red wine, stirring well until the mixture is thoroughly blended and smooth. Add the hare pieces and leave to marinate at room temperature for 6 hours or overnight, basting occasionally.

To make the pastry, sift the flour, baking powder and salt into a large mixing bowl. Rub in the suet with your fingertips. Mix in the water and make a soft dough. Using your hands, knead the dough lightly until it is smooth and elastic.

Turn the dough out on to a lightly

Hearty and warming, Hare Pudding is a filling meal flavoured with wine.

floured board. With a floured rolling pin, roll out the dough to a large circle about 1cm (½in) thick. Cut a triangle (about one-third of the diameter) out of the circle and reserve it. Line a 1.5 litre (2½ pint) pudding basin [1½ quart round casserole] with the large piece of dough. Dampen the cut edges and bring them together. Trim the edges of the dough so that it is even with the rim.

Pour the meat and marinade into the lined container. Lightly knead the reserved triangle with the trimmings. On a lightly floured board, roll out a circle large enough to cover the top of the container. Dampen the edges and place the circle on top of the meat. Press the edges of the dough together to seal them.

Cut out a circle of aluminium foil 13cm (5in) wider in diameter than the rim of the container. Lightly grease the foil with the oil. Make a 5cm (2in) pleat across the centre of the circle and place it, greased side down, over the container. Tie it on securely with string, leaving a loop with which to lift the pudding out of the cooker, when it has finished cooking.

Remove the trivet. Pour the boiling water into the cooker. Replace the trivet. Place the pudding on the trivet and close the cooker but do not fit the indicator weight. Pre-steam for 20 minutes. This means that the water simmers and steam escapes through the vent.

Position the indicator weight. Bring to LOW pressure and cook for $1\frac{1}{4}$ hours.

Allow the pressure to reduce at room temperature.

Remove the pudding from the cooker and discard the foil. Serve immediately.

Below : Game Stew can be made with hare or venison.

GAME STEW

4 servings
30 minutes HIGH pressure
5 minutes HIGH pressure

Metric/Imperial

1kg (2lb) hare or venison, cut into cubes
50g (2oz) butter
1 bay leaf
1 large green pepper, white pith removed, seeded and chopped
175g (6oz) button mushrooms, wiped clean
175g (6oz) small white onions, peeled and left whole

MARINADE
2 medium-sized carrots, scraped and sliced
1 large onion, finely sliced
2 garlic cloves, crushed
1 tablespoon chopped fresh parsley
400ml (15fl oz) dry red wine
150ml (5floz) beef stock
50ml (2fl oz) olive oil
$\frac{1}{2}$ teaspoon salt
$\frac{1}{2}$ teaspoon black pepper

American

2lb hare or venison, cut into cubes
4 tablespoons butter
1 bay leaf
1 large green pepper, white membrane removed, seeded and chopped
6oz button mushrooms, wiped clean
6oz small white onions, peeled and left whole
MARINADE
2 medium-sized carrots, scraped and sliced
1 large onion, finely sliced
2 garlic cloves, crushed
1 tablespoon chopped fresh parsley
2 cups dry red wine
$\frac{1}{2}$ cup beef stock
$\frac{1}{4}$ cup olive oil
$\frac{1}{2}$ teaspoon salt
$\frac{1}{2}$ teaspoon black pepper

In a large, shallow dish, combine all of the marinade ingredients. Add the meat and leave it to marinate at room temperature for 8 hours or overnight, basting occasionally.

Remove the meat from the marinade and dry thoroughly on kitchen paper towels. Reserve the marinade.

Remove the trivet. Melt the butter in the open cooker over moderate heat. When the foam subsides, add the meat and cook, turning occasionally, for 5 minutes or until the meat is browned on all sides. Add the bay leaf and the reserved marinade. Bring to HIGH pressure and cook for 30 minutes.

Allow the pressure to reduce at room temperature.

Stir in the green pepper, mushrooms and onions. Bring to HIGH pressure and cook for 5 minutes.

Allow the pressure to reduce at room temperature.

Transfer the stew to a warmed serving dish, removing and discarding the bay leaf. Serve immediately.

DESSERTS

With all the hurry of modern life, desserts and puddings are among the first things discarded by the busy cook. Steamed sponge and suet crust puddings, crammed full of fruit and flavourings, fill up and warm up even the hungriest, coldest family in the winter. These used to take such a long time to cook, often as much as three hours, and needed constant attention to make sure the water had not boiled dry, to say nothing of ending up with a kitchen like a Turkish bath. Steamed puddings take up to one hour in a pressure cooker, even the rich mixture of Christmas pudding takes no more than two hours. There is no need to watch the saucepan all the time and the kitchen does not suffer with condensation.

Steam puddings no longer require the planning of a battle strategist and can be made easily any evening of the week, no matter how busy you are.

Steam puddings are not the only type of dessert that can be succesfully pressure cooked. Creamy rice puddings and light tempting custards are ideally suited to pressure cooking too. They take about one-third of the time and you can guarantee perfect results.

Fresh fruit can be cooked in a matter of moments and this can

Re-discover the delights of desserts and puddings with your pressure cooker! Below : Pots de Crème au Luxe.

be very helpful if you have unexpected guests. Even dried fruit needs no more than 10 minutes soaking and up to 10 minutes cooking.

General hints – steamed puddings
Check that the pudding basin [round casserole] fits into the cooker easily. It can be made of any heatproof material such as ovenproof glass, metal, earthenware or boilable plastic. Add 5 minutes extra to the cooking time if you are using earthenware or glass. Grease it well before you put the mixture into it and do not fill it more than two-thirds full as puddings expand during cooking.

Do not use a fitted lid (sometimes supplied with boilable plastic containers). Cut out a circle of greaseproof or waxed paper about 10cm (4in) bigger in diameter than the rim of the container. Lightly grease this with ½ teaspoon butter. Cut a circle of aluminium foil the same size and place the two circles together, buttered side of the paper away from the foil. Make a 3cm (1in) pleat across the centre. Firmly tie the two circles, foil uppermost, on to the pudding, leaving a loop of string with which to lift the pudding out, when cooked.

Place the trivet in the cooker and at least 1.5 litres (2½ pints) [6 cups] boiling water. A little lemon juice or vinegar added to the water will prevent the cooker discolouring in hard water areas. Stand the pudding on the trivet. Close the cooker but do not fit the indicator weight. Pre-steam the pudding (for the time see the chart below). This means that the water simmers and steam escapes through the vent. This allows the raising agents to work so that the pudding will be light and fluffy. Do not turn the heat up high during pre-steaming as too much water will be lost through evporation and the cooker will boil dry during the main cooking.

LOW pressure is used for steamed puddings.

Allow the pressure to reduce at room temperature when the cooking is completed.

Cooking time – steamed puddings (LOW pressure)

Normal cooking time	Pre-steaming	Time at LOW pressure
30 minutes	5 minutes	7 minutes
1 hour	15 minutes	25 minutes
1½-2 hours	15 minutes	35 minutes
2-3 hours	20 minutes	50-60 minutes

General hints – milk puddings
Milk puddings are cooked directly in the cooker, without the trivet. This makes them especially thick, creamy and rich. Do not fill the cooker more than half full.

Cook at MEDIUM pressure and allow the pressure to reduce at room temperature (a minimum of 5 minutes) after cooking. Transfer to a warmed serving dish. You can, if you like, brown the top under the grill.

General hints – egg puddings
These were traditionally made by steaming and this produces light fluffy custards and crèmes.

Cook in separate dishes, or one large dish, on the trivet at

HIGH pressure for about one-third of the normal time. Allow the pressure to reduce at room temperature. This is very important or the egg will curdle and not set.

General hints – fresh fruit
Time depends on the kind of fruit and on its ripeness. Soft fruits are best cooked in a heatproof dish as they have a high proportion of juice. Add a small quantity of sugar if liked.

Cooking times

Apple slices	10 minutes MEDIUM pressure. Allow pressure to reduce at room temperature.
Apricots	Bring to HIGH pressure and reduce pressure immediately with cold water.
Blackcurrants	Bring to MEDIUM pressure and reduce pressure immediately with cold water.
Cherries	Bring to HIGH pressure and reduce pressure immediately with cold water.
Damsons	Bring to HIGH pressure and reduce pressure immediately with cold water.
Gooseberries	Bring to MEDIUM pressure and reduce pressure immediately with cold water.
Greengages	Bring to HIGH pressure and reduce pressure immediately with cold water.
Loganberries	Bring to MEDIUM pressure and reduce pressure immediately with cold water.
Peaches	5 minutes HIGH pressure. Reduce pressure with cold water.
Pears	5-10 minutes HIGH pressure. Reduce pressure with cold water.
Rhubarb	1 minute MEDIUM pressure. Allow pressure to reduce at room temperature.

General hints – dried fruit
Wash the fruit and put it in a bowl. Pour over 600ml (1 pint) [2½ cups] of water for every 500g (1lb) of fruit. Cover and leave to soak for 10 minutes.

As dried fruit expands during cooking do not fill the cooker more than half full. Use a minimum of 300ml (10fl oz) [1¼ cups] of liquid.

Cook at HIGH pressure and allow the pressure to reduce at room temperature.

Cooking time – dried fruit (HIGH pressure)

Apples	6 minutes
Apricots	3 minutes
Figs	10 minutes
Peaches	5 minutes
Pears	10 minutes
Prunes	10 minutes

DESSERTS

POTS DE CREME AU LUXE: SMALL CUSTARD CREAMS

6 servings
6 minutes HIGH pressure

Metric/Imperial

600ml (1 pint) double cream
5 egg yolks
1 egg
3 tablespoons sugar
2 tablespoons strong black coffee
2 tablespoons brandy
300ml ($\frac{1}{2}$ pint) water

American

$2\frac{1}{2}$ cups heavy cream
5 egg yolks
1 egg
3 tablespoons sugar
2 tablespoons strong black coffee
2 tablespoons brandy
$1\frac{1}{4}$ cups water

In a small saucepan, heat the cream over low heat. When the cream is hot but not boiling, remove the pan from the heat and set aside.

In a medium-sized mixing bowl, beat the egg yolks, egg, sugar, black coffee and brandy together with a wooden spoon, until they are just combined. Stirring constantly with a wooden spoon, gradually pour the cream into the egg mixture, beating until they are well blended. Strain the mixture into another bowl.

Pour the mixture into 6 small ramekin dishes or custard cups. Alternatively, use a single large dish, but check that it fits into the cooker before pouring the mixture into it. Cover each one with aluminium foil.

Remove the trivet. Pour the water into the cooker and replace the trivet. Arrange the dishes or cups on the trivet. Bring to HIGH pressure and cook for 6 minutes.

Allow the pressure to reduce at room temperature.

Leave the custard to cool completely then chill in the refrigerator for 30 minutes.

Do not try to hurry the process of cooling as the eggs may cause the custard to curdle and completely spoil the dish.

Remove the dishes or cups from the refrigerator and serve immediately.

ORANGE CUSTARD

4 servings
5 minutes HIGH pressure

Metric/Imperial

2 sugar cubes
1 orange
3 egg yolks
50g (2oz) sugar
1 tablespoon brandy
300ml ($\frac{1}{2}$ pint) single cream
300ml ($\frac{1}{2}$ pint) water

American

2 sugar cubes
1 orange
3 egg yolks
$\frac{1}{4}$ cup sugar
1 tablespoon brandy
$1\frac{1}{4}$ cups light cream
$1\frac{1}{4}$ cups water

Rub the sugar cubes all over the orange until they have absorbed all the zest. Put the sugar cubes into a medium-sized mixing bowl, crush them with the back of a wooden spoon and set aside for use later.

Cut the orange in half and squeeze out the juice. Set aside. Discard the orange halves.

Add the egg yolks and the sugar to the sugar cubes and mix well with a wooden spoon. Stir in the brandy and the orange juice. Set aside.

In a small saucepan, heat the cream over low heat. When it is hot, but not boiling, remove the pan from the heat. Gradually stir the cream into the egg yolk mixture, beating with a wooden spoon until they are well blended. Strain the mixture into another bowl.

Pour the mixture into 4 small ramekin dishes or custard cups. Cover each one with aluminium foil.

Remove the trivet. Pour the water into the cooker and replace the trivet. Arrange the dishes or cups on the trivet. Bring to HIGH pressure and cook for 5 minutes.

Allow the pressure to reduce at room temperature.

Remove the dishes or cups from the cooker and serve immediately, if you are serving the custards hot. If you are serving them cold, allow them to cool completely and then chill in the refrigerator for 30 minutes before serving.

ROLY-POLY WITH DRIED FRUIT

4-6 servings
20 minutes pre-steaming
1 hour LOW pressure

Metric/Imperial

225g (8oz) flour
1 teaspoon salt
2 tablespoons sugar
2 teaspoons baking powder
75g (3oz) shredded suet
10-12 tablespoons water
50g (2oz) currants
125g (4oz) raisins
50g (2oz) chopped mixed candied peel
1 tablespoon milk
1 teaspoon butter
1.5 litres ($2\frac{1}{2}$ pints) boiling water

American

$1\frac{3}{4}$ cups flour
1 teaspoon salt
2 tablespoons sugar
2 teaspoons baking powder
3oz shredded suet
10-12 tablespoons water
$\frac{1}{4}$ cup currants
$\frac{2}{3}$ cup raisins
$\frac{1}{4}$ cup chopped mixed candied peel
1 tablespoon milk
1 teaspoon butter
6 cups boiling water

Sift the flour, salt, sugar and baking powder into a large mixing bowl. Stir in the suet. Gradually add 10 tablespoons of the water to the mixture and knead lightly until the dough is light and pliable. Add more water, one spoonful at a time, if the dough is too stiff.

On a lightly floured board, roll out the dough to a rectangle about $\frac{1}{2}$cm ($\frac{1}{4}$in) thick. Sprinkle the currants, raisins and peel evenly over the surface, leaving a margin of about $\frac{1}{2}$cm ($\frac{1}{4}$in) all around the edges. With a pastry brush, brush the edges with the milk.

Roll up the dough along its length, pressing the edges together to seal them. Cut out a rectangle of greaseproof or waxed paper about 10cm (4in) longer than the circumference of the pastry roll and about 10cm (4in) wider. Using the teaspoon of butter, lightly grease the paper. Cut out a rectangle of aluminium foil the same size.

Place the two rectangles together, the

DESSERTS

greased side of the paper away from the foil and, holding them firmly, make a 3cm (1in) pleat across the middle. Wrap the pudding in the paper and foil, greased side towards the pastry, tucking in the ends securely.

Remove the trivet. Pour in the boiling water and replace the trivet. Place the pudding on the trivet. Close the cooker but do not fit the indicator weight. Pre-steam for 20 minutes. This means that the water simmers and steam escapes through the vent.

Position the indicator weight. Bring to LOW pressure. Cook for 1 hour.

Allow the pressure to reduce at room temperature.

Lift out the pudding and unwrap it. Transfer it to a warmed serving dish and serve immediately.

FIG PUDDING

4 servings
20 minutes pre-steaming
1 hour LOW pressure

Metric/Imperial

1 tablespoon butter

175g (6oz) dried figs, stalks removed and chopped
75g (3oz) soft brown sugar
75g (3oz) dry breadcrumbs
50g (2oz) finely chopped suet
75g (3oz) flour
¼ teaspoon salt
½ teaspoon ground cinnamon
2 eggs
150ml (5fl oz) milk
juice of ½ lemon
1.5 litres (2½ pints) boiling water

American

1 tablespoon butter
6oz dried figs, stalks removed and chopped
½ cup soft brown sugar
1⅛ cups dry breadcrumbs
2oz finely chopped suet
½ cup flour
¼ teaspoon salt
½ teaspoon ground cinnamon
2 eggs
⅔ cup milk
juice of ½ lemon
6 cups boiling water

Grease a 1 litre (2 pint) pudding basin

Roly Poly Pudding with dried fruit contains currants, raisins and tangy candied peel.

[1 quart round casserole] with half of the butter. Set aside.

In a large mixing bowl, combine the figs, sugar, breadcrumbs and suet. Sift the flour, salt and cinnamon into the bowl. Add the eggs and half the milk. Beat well to combine the mixture. Stir in the remaining milk and the lemon juice.

Spoon the mixture into the container. Cut out a circle of greaseproof or waxed paper about 10cm (4in) wider in diameter than the rim of the container. With the remaining butter lightly grease the paper circle. Cut out a circle of aluminium foil the same size as the paper circle. Place the two circles together, with the greased side of the paper circle away from the foil. Holding them firmly together, make a 5cm (2in) pleat. Put the circles over the pudding foil uppermost. Securely tie with string, leaving a loop with which to lift the pudding out of the cooker, when cooked.

Remove the trivet. Pour the boiling

71

water into the cooker and replace the trivet. Position the pudding on the trivet and close the cooker but do not fit the indicator weight. Pre-steam for 20 minutes. This means that the water simmers and steam escapes through the vent.

Position the indicator weight and bring to LOW pressure. Cook for 1 hour.

Allow the pressure to reduce at room temperature.

Remove the pudding from the cooker. Remove and discard the paper and foil circles. Place a warmed serving plate, inverted, over the pudding and reverse the two. The pudding should slide out easily. Serve immediately.

CHRISTMAS PUDDING

2 puddings
20 minutes pre-steaming
2 hours HIGH pressure

Metric/Imperial

25g (1oz) butter
225g (8oz) self-raising flour
1 teaspoon salt
1 teaspoon grated nutmeg
1 teaspoon ground cinnamon
1 teaspoon ground cloves
350g (12oz) fresh breadcrumbs
350g (12oz) suet, shredded
450g (1lb) light brown sugar
500g (1lb) currants
500g (1lb) sultanas
1kg (2lb) raisins
125g (4oz) candied peel, chopped
50g (2oz) glacé cherries, chopped
50g (2oz) blanched almonds, slivered
2 medium-sized cooking apples,
    peeled, cored and shredded
finely grated rind and juice of 1 orange
finely grated rind and juice of 1 lemon
6 eggs
150ml (5fl oz) milk
50ml (2fl oz) brandy for each pudding
1.8 litres (3 pints) boiling water for
    each pudding

American

2 tablespoons butter
1¾ cups self-raising cake flour
1 teaspoon salt
1 teaspoon grated nutmeg
1 teaspoon ground cinnamon
1 teaspoon ground cloves

6 cups fresh breadcrumbs
12oz suet, shredded
1lb light brown sugar
1lb currants
1lb golden raisins
2lb raisins
4oz candied peel, chopped
2oz glacé cherries, chopped
2oz blanched almonds, slivered
2 medium-sized cooking apples,
    peeled, cored and shredded
finely grated rind and juice of 1 orange
finely grated rind and juice of 1 lemon
6 eggs
⅔ cup milk
¼ cup brandy for each pudding
7½ cups boiling water for each pudding

Generously grease two 1.75-litre (3-pint) pudding basins [2-quart round casseroles], using half the butter. Set aside.

In a very large mixing bowl, sift together the flour, salt, nutmeg, cinnamon and cloves. Add the breadcrumbs, suet, sugar, currants, sultanas [golden raisins], raisins, candied peel, cherries and almonds. With a spoon, blend the ingredients well together. Stir in the shredded apple and the grated orange and lemon rinds.

In a small bowl lightly beat the eggs with a fork. Stir the milk, and orange and lemon juice into the eggs. Add the egg and milk mixture to the large bowl and fold in until the dry ingredients are thoroughly moistened.

Spoon the mixture into the prepared containers, packing it in well and doming the top slightly.

Cut out two circles of greaseproof or waxed paper about 10cm (4in) wider in diameter than the rims of the containers. Grease the circles with the remaining butter. Cut out two circles of aluminium foil the same size as the paper circles. Place one paper circle and foil circle together, the buttered side of the paper away from the foil. Holding them firmly together, make a 5cm (2in) pleat. Place the pleated circles over one pudding and securely tie with string, leaving a loop with which to lift the pudding out of the cooker, when cooked.

Cover the other pudding with the other paper and foil circles in the same way.

Cook one pudding at a time.

Remove the trivet. Pour in the boiling

water and replace the trivet. Position one pudding on the trivet and close the cooker but do not fit the indicator weight. Pre-steam for 20 minutes. This means that the water simmers and steam escapes through the vent.

Position the indicator weight and bring to HIGH pressure. Cook for 2 hours.

Allow the pressure to reduce at room temperature.

Lift the pudding out of the cooker and set aside to cool for 1 hour.

Cook the other pudding in the same way.

Cut out two circles of greaseproof or waxed paper and two circles of aluminium foil, as before. Pleat them as before. Remove and discard the paper and foil circles from the puddings and replace them with fresh ones, tying them on securely with string. Store the puddings in a cool dry place for at least 3 weeks so that they mature.

To prepare a pudding for eating at Christmas, remove the trivet from the cooker and pour in 1.8 litres (3 pints) [7½ cups] boiling water. Replace the trivet and position the pudding on it. Close the cooker but do not fit the indicator weight. Pre-steam for 20 minutes.

Position the indicator weight and bring to HIGH pressure. Cook for 1 hour.

Allow the pressure to reduce at room temperature.

Remove the pudding from the cooker. Place a warmed serving plate, inverted, over the pudding and reverse the two. The pudding should slide out easily.

Warm the brandy in a small saucepan over low heat. Pour the warmed brandy over the pudding and set alight with a match. Serve immediately while the pudding is flaming.

FLUMMERY

4 servings
12 minutes HIGH pressure

Metric/Imperial

25g (1oz) butter
300ml (10fl oz) milk
300ml (10fl oz) double cream
125g (4oz) round-grain rice, washed
50g (2oz) sugar
1 tablespoon lemon rind

1 teaspoon ground cinnamon

American

2 tablespoons butter
1¼ cups milk
1¼ cups heavy cream
⅔ cups short-grained rice, washed
¼ cup sugar
1 tablespoon lemon rind
1 teaspoon ground cinnamon

Remove the trivet. Melt the butter in the open cooker over moderate heat. Increase the heat to high and pour in the milk and the cream and bring to the boil. Add the rice, sugar, lemon rind and cinnamon. Bring the milk and cream back to the boil, stirring constantly. Reduce the heat to low so that the milk is simmering.

Close the cooker and fit the indicator weight. Bring to HIGH pressure, without altering the heat. This will take a little longer than usual. Cook for 12 minutes.

Allow the pressure to reduce at room temperature.

Pour the mixture into a soufflé dish.

Allow it to cool at room temperature and then place the dish in the refrigerator to chill for 3 hours or until the flummery is set. Serve cold.

PRUNES IN RED WINE

6 servings
10 minutes HIGH pressure

Metric/Imperial

500g (1lb) prunes, soaked in hot water for 10 minutes and drained
300ml (10fl oz) dry red wine
50g (2oz) sugar
1 teaspoon lemon juice
1 teaspoon grated lemon rind

American

1lb prunes, soaked in hot water for 10 minutes and drained
1¼ cups dry red wine
¼ cup sugar
1 teaspoon lemon juice
1 teaspoon grated lemon rind

Remove the trivet. Put the prunes and

Flummery is the unusual name for this delectable summer dessert. It contains rice, cream, lemon and cinnamon and should be served chilled, topped with whipped cream. This old English recipe would be equally suitable for a hot summer's day or as a delicious dessert to follow a hearty stew in winter.

red wine in the cooker. Bring to HIGH pressure and cook for 10 minutes.

Allow the pressure to reduce at room temperature.

With a slotted spoon, lift out the prunes and divide them among six individual serving dishes.

Place the open cooker over high heat and stir in the sugar and lemon juice. Bring the liquid to the boil, stirring constantly.

Reduce the heat to low and simmer the sauce for 20 minutes or until the liquid has reduced by about one-third.

Pour the syrup over the prunes. Sprinkle a little grated lemon rind over each dish. Set aside to cool. When the dishes have cooled completely, place them in the refrigerator to chill for 1 hour before serving.

DESSERTS

GINGER PUDDING

6 servings
20 minutes pre-steaming
50 minutes LOW pressure

Metric/Imperial

125g (4oz) plus 3 teaspoons butter
125g (4oz) sugar
2 eggs
2 tablespoons sour cream
175g (6oz) self-raising flour
1½ teaspoons ground ginger
2 tablespoons finely chopped preserved
   ginger
1½ litres (2½ pints) boiling water

American

1 stick plus 3 teaspoons butter
½ cup sugar
2 eggs
2 tablespoons sour cream
1½ cups self-raising cake flour
1½ teaspoons ground ginger
2 tablespoons finely chopped
   preserved ginger
6 cups boiling water

Grease a 1 litre (2 pint) pudding basin [1 quart round casserole] with 2 teaspoons of the butter. Set aside.

In a medium-sized mixing bowl, cream 125g (4oz) [1 stick] of the butter with a wooden spoon until it is soft. Add the sugar and beat the mixture until it is pale and fluffy. Beat the eggs in, one at a time. Stir in the sour cream. Sift the flour and ginger on to the creamed mixture and cut and fold it in with a metal spoon. Gently stir in the chopped ginger.

Spoon the mixture into the container and smooth the top with a spoon. Cut out a circle of greaseproof or waxed paper about 10cm (4in) wider in diameter than the rim of the container. Using the remaining teaspoon of butter, lightly grease the paper circle. Cut out a circle of aluminium foil the same size as the paper circle. Place the two circles together, buttered side away from the foil. Holding them firmly together, make a 5cm (2in) pleat across the centre. Place the circles, buttered side down, over the pudding. Securely tie with string, leaving a loop with which to lift the pudding out of the cooker, when cooked.

Remove the trivet. Pour the boiling water into the cooker and replace the trivet. Position the pudding on the trivet, and close the cooker but do not fit the indicator weight. Pre-steam for 20 minutes. This means that the water simmers and steam escapes through the vent.

Position the indicator weight and bring to LOW pressure, and cook for 50 minutes.

Allow the pressure to reduce at room temperature.

Remove the pudding from the cooker. Remove and discard the paper and foil circles. Place a warmed serving dish, inverted, over the pudding and reverse the two. The pudding should slide out easily. Serve immediately.

PEAR CONDE

6 servings
12 minutes HIGH pressure

Metric/Imperial

1 teaspoon vegetable oil
25g (1oz) butter
900ml (1½ pints) milk
125g (4oz) round-grain rice, washed
275g (10oz) sugar
⅛ teaspoon salt
1 teaspoon vanilla essence
6 egg yolks, lightly beaten
1kg (2lb) firm pears, peeled, halved and
   cored
225ml (8fl oz) water
3 tablespoons brandy
4 glacé cherries, halved

American

2 tablespoons butter
3¾ cups milk
⅔ cup short-grained rice
1¼ cups sugar
⅛ teaspoon salt
1 teaspoon vanilla
6 egg yolks, lightly beaten
2lb firm pears, peeled, halved and
   cored
1 cup water
3 tablespoons brandy
4 glacé cherries, halved

Lightly grease a 1 litre (2 pint) [1 quart] soufflé dish with the oil. Set aside.

Remove the trivet. Melt the butter in the open cooker over moderate heat.

Increase the heat to high and pour in the milk. Bring the milk to the boil and then add the rice, 50g (2oz) [¼ cup] of the sugar, salt and vanilla essence. Bring the milk back to the boil, stirring constantly. Reduce the heat to low so that the milk is simmering.

Close the cooker and fit the indicator weight. Bring the cooker to HIGH pressure, without altering the heat. This will take a little longer than usual. Cook for 12 minutes.

Allow the pressure to reduce at room temperature.

Stir the egg yolks into the rice mixture. Place the open cooker over low heat. Cook gently, stirring constantly, for 3 minutes. Set aside to cool.

With a sharp knife, cut about one quarter of the pear halves into thin slices. Set aside.

When the rice mixture is cool, spoon about one-third of it into the prepared soufflé dish. Place half the pear slices on top. Continue making layers until all the ingredients are used up, ending with a layer of the rice mixture. Cover the dish with aluminium foil and place it in the refrigerator to chill for 2 hours or until the rice mixture is firm.

Meanwhile, make the sauce. In a medium-sized saucepan, dissolve the remaining sugar in the water over moderate heat, stirring constantly. Add the remaining pear halves. Reduce the heat to low and simmer for 12 to 15 minutes, or until the pears are tender. Remove the pan from the heat.

With a slotted spoon, remove half of the pear halves from the pan and set them aside.

Purée the remaining pear halves with the syrup in an electric blender. Alternatively, stir the mixture through a strainer with a wooden spoon to make a purée. Return the purée to the pan and return the pan to high heat. Boil the sauce for 3 minutes.

Remove the pan from the heat and stir in the brandy. Pour the sauce into a bowl and set aside to cool. When it is completely cool, place the bowl in the refrigerator to chill for 30 minutes.

Remove the soufflé dish from the refrigerator. Remove and discard the

An impressive French classic dessert, Pear Condé is a mould of pears and rice with a delicious brandy sauce, and garnished with pear slices and cherries.

aluminium foil. Place a serving dish, inverted, over the soufflé dish and reverse the two. The pudding should slide out easily. Arrange the reserved pear halves on top and around the sides. Decorate with the cherries. Serve the sauce separately.

APPLES in BRANDY and VERMOUTH

4 servings
4 minutes HIGH pressure

Metric/Imperial

4 medium-sized cooking apples, washed and cored
25g (1oz) plus 4 teaspoons butter
2 tablespoons caster sugar
125ml (4fl oz) dry white vermouth
125ml (4fl oz) water
75ml (3fl oz) brandy
300ml ($\frac{1}{2}$ pint) hot water
4 slices white bread, crusts removed and cut into circles about 1cm ($\frac{1}{2}$in) thick and 8cm (3in) in diameter
2 tablespoons redcurrant jelly

American

4 medium-sized cooking apples, washed and cored
2 tablespoons plus 4 teaspoons butter
2 tablespoons extra fine sugar
$\frac{1}{2}$ cup dry white vermouth
$\frac{1}{2}$ cup water
$\frac{1}{3}$ cup brandy
1$\frac{1}{4}$ cups hot water
4 slices white bread, crusts removed and cut into circles about $\frac{1}{2}$in thick and 3in in diameter
2 tablespoons redcurrant jelly

Using a sharp knife, make shallow slits all around the apples, starting from the centre and extending halfway down the sides.

Put one teaspoon of butter in the centre of each apple and place them upright in a medium-sized, heatproof dish. Sprinkle over the sugar and pour in the vermouth, cold water and 2 tablespoons of the brandy. Cover the dish with aluminium foil.

Remove the trivet and pour the hot water into the cooker. Replace the trivet and position the dish on it. Bring to HIGH pressure and cook for 4 minutes.

Allow the pressure to reduce at room temperature.

Meanwhile, melt the remaining butter in a medium-sized frying-pan over moderate heat. When the foam subsides, add the bread slices and fry for 1 or 2 minutes or until they are golden. With a spatula or a fish slice, remove the fried bread from the pan and drain on kitchen paper towels. Arrange them on a warmed serving dish.

Carefully lift the baking dish from the cooker and, with a slotted spoon, place one apple on each slice of bread. Set aside and keep warm.

Pour the cooking liquid from the baking dish into a medium-sized saucepan. Set the pan over high heat and add the remaining brandy and the redcurrant jelly. Cook, stirring constantly, for 5 to 7 minutes, or until the sauce has reduced by about half.

Remove the pan from the heat and spoon the sauce over the apples. Serve immediately.

DUCHESS PUDDING

4-6 servings
15 minutes pre-steaming
35 minutes LOW pressure

Metric/Imperial

125g (4oz) plus 2 teaspoons butter
125g (4oz) sugar
2 eggs
175g (6oz) self-raising flour
50g (2oz) raisins
50g (2oz) almonds, chopped
$\frac{1}{4}$ teaspoon almond essence
1 to 3 tablespoons milk
1.5 litres (2$\frac{1}{2}$ pints) boiling water

American

1 stick plus 2 teaspoons butter
$\frac{1}{2}$ cup sugar
2 eggs
1$\frac{1}{2}$ cups self-raising cake flour
$\frac{1}{3}$ cup raisins
$\frac{1}{3}$ cup almonds, chopped
$\frac{1}{4}$ teaspoon almond essence
1 to 3 tablespoons milk
6 cups boiling water

With 1 teaspoon of the butter, grease a 1 litre (2 pint) pudding basin [1 quart round casserole]. Set aside.

In a medium-sized mixing bowl, cream 125g (4oz) [1 stick] of the butter and the sugar together with a wooden spoon until the mixture is pale and fluffy.

Add one of the eggs with a tablespoon of flour. Beat briskly. Add the second egg and another tablespoon of flour. Fold the remaining flour, the raisins and the almonds into the mixture.

Add the almond essence and enough milk to make the batter a dropping consistency. Spoon the batter into the container, doming the top slightly.

Cut out a circle of greaseproof or waxed paper about 10cm (4in) wider in diameter than the rim of the container. Grease the circle with the remaining butter. Cut out a circle of aluminium foil the same size as the paper circle. Place the circles together, the buttered side of the paper away from the foil. Holding the two circles firmly together, make a 5cm (2in) pleat. Place the circles, foil uppermost, over the pudding. Securely tie with string, leaving a loop with which to lift the pudding out of the cooker, when cooked.

Remove the trivet. Pour the water into the cooker and replace the trivet. Position the pudding on the trivet and close the cooker but do not fit the indicator weight. Pre-steam for 15 minutes. This means the water simmers and steam escapes through the vent.

Position the indicator weight and bring to LOW pressure. Cook for 35 minutes.

Allow the pressure to reduce at room temperature.

Remove the pudding from the cooker. Remove and discard the foil and paper circles. Place a warmed serving plate, inverted, over the pudding and reverse the two. The pudding should slide out easily. Serve immediately.

PRESERVES

A pressure cooker is excellent for making jams, jellies, marmalades and chutneys. The initial softening of the fruit can be done in a fraction of the normal time. The sugar is dissolved and the jam or chutney is boiled until it is ready in the open cooker. Very soft fruits, such as strawberries, are not suitable for jam making in the pressure cooker.

General hints – jam

Wash and dry the fruit. Only use fresh undamaged fruit. Remove the trivet and put the fruit and a minimum of 300ml (10fl oz) [1¼ cups] of water in the cooker. (See the individual recipes for quantities). Bring to MEDIUM pressure and cook for about 5 minutes. Allow the pressure to reduce at room temperature. Add 500g (1lb) [2 cups] sugar for every 500g (1lb) of fruit used. Stir in the open cooker over low heat until all the sugar is dissolved. It is very important that you do not boil the jam until all the sugar has dissolved, otherwise the jam will not set and the sugar will burn into a filthy mess on the bottom of the cooker.

Increase the heat to high and boil the jam rapidly until setting point is reached. To test for setting point, remove the cooker from the heat and put a spoon of the jam on a cold saucer. Cool it rapidly. If the surface sets and wrinkles when pushed with your finger, the jam is ready. If you have a sugar [candy] thermometer, when the temperature reaches 105°C (220°F), the jam is ready.

Skim off any foam with a metal spoon. If the jam contains whole fruit, allow it to stand for 10 minutes or until a skin forms, otherwise the fruit will rise to the top of the jars. Ladle the jam into clean, warm, dry jars and put a circle of waxed paper in each one. Wipe inside and outside the rims with a warm damp cloth to remove any stickiness. When cool, cover with cellophane fastened with elastic bands. Alternatively, seal with parafin wax. Label and store in a cool, dry place.

General hints – marmalades

Marmalade is made from citrus fruits and includes the peel. Put the fruit and peel in the cooker. Tie the pips [pits] in cheesecloth or muslin and add these. Add at least 300ml (10fl oz) [1¼ cups] water. Bring to HIGH pressure and cook for 10 to 15 minutes. Allow the pressure to reduce at room temperature. Remove and discard the bag of pips [pits]. Add 1kg (2lb) [4 cups] sugar for every 500g (1lb) of fruit. Proceed as for jam.

General hints – jellies

Jams and marmalades can be made in jelly form. Pressure cook as before. Then pour the mixture through a scalded jelly bag or large square of cheesecloth placed over a large bowl. Leave to strain for at least 12 hours. Do not squeeze the bag as this can make the jelly cloudy.
Add 450g (1lb) [2 cups] of sugar for every 600ml (1 pint) [2½ cups] liquid and proceed as for jam.

Preserving is easy with a pressure cooker. Peach Jam (above) is one of the many delicious jams you could make.

General hints – chutney

Chutney can be made with all sorts of fruits.
Place the fruit in the cooker with half the vinegar and bring to HIGH pressure for the required time (see individual recipes). Allow the pressure to reduce at room temperature.
Stir the sugar into the open cooker over low heat. Do not boil until the sugar has dissolved otherwise the sugar will burn on to the bottom of the cooker, spoil the flavour of the chutney and make a disgusting mess. Add the remaining vinegar.
Boil rapidly, stirring occasionally, until the chutney is thick. Ladle the chutney into warm, dry, clean jars. Wipe the inside and outside of the rims with a warm, damp cloth to remove any stickiness. Place a circle of waxed paper in each jar. If you are using vacuum-sealed lids fit these immediately or screw on the tops.
When cool, label the jars and store in a cool dry place for at least 6 weeks before eating.

REDCURRANT JELLY

about 1.5kg (3lb)
5 minutes MEDIUM pressure

Metric/Imperial

1kg (2lb) redcurrants, trimmed
300ml (10fl oz) water
sugar

American

2lb redcurrants, trimmed
1¼ cups water
sugar

Remove the trivet. Put the redcurrants and water in the cooker. Bring to MEDIUM pressure and cook for 5 minutes.

Allow the pressure to reduce at room temperature.

Hang a scalded jelly bag or large square of cheesecloth over a large bowl. Pour the redcurrants into the cloth. Allow the juice to drain for at least 12 hours. Do not squeeze the bag as this might make the jelly cloudy. When all the juice has drained, discard the fruit

Make the redcurrant jelly you will need to accompany roast lamb or the delicious game recipes given earlier in this book.

pulp remaining in the jelly bag.

Measure the juice and return it to the rinsed cooker. Add 450g (1lb) [2 cups] of sugar to every 600ml (1 pint) [2½ cups] of juice. Stir in the sugar in the open cooker over low heat. When the sugar has dissolved increase the heat to high. Boil briskly, without stirring, for about 20 minutes or until the jelly has reached setting point.

To test for setting point, remove the cooker from the heat and put a spoonful of jam on a cold saucer. Cool quickly. If the surface is set and wrinkles when pushed with your finger, the jelly is ready. If you have a sugar [candy] thermometer, when the temperature reaches 105°C (220°F), the jelly is ready.

Skim the foam of the surface of the jelly with a metal spoon. Ladle the jelly into warmed, clean, dry jars to within 1.5cm (½in) of the top. Wipe inside and outside the rims with a damp cloth to remove any stickiness. Place a waxed

paper circle in each jar. When the jars are cool, cover with cellophane fastened with elastic bands. Alternatively, seal with parafin wax. Label the jars and store in a cool, dark, dry place.

DARK SEVILLE MARMALADE

about 4kg (8lb)
15 minutes HIGH pressure

Metric/Imperial

1.5kg (3lb) Seville oranges
juice of 2 lemons
3 litres (5 pints) water
3kg (6lb) brown sugar

American

3lb Seville oranges
juice of 2 lemons
12½ cups water
6lb brown sugar

Scrub the oranges. Cut them in half and squeeze out the juice. Remove the pith [white membrane] from the skin. Tie the pith [white membrane], pips

[pits] and any coarse tissue in a piece of cheesecloth. Chop up the peel into small slivers.

Remove the trivet. Put the peel, cheesecloth containing the pips [pits] the orange and lemon juice and half the water into the cooker. Bring to HIGH pressure and cook for 15 minutes.

Allow the pressure to reduce at room temperature. Remove the cheesecloth bag, squeezing it well against the side of the cooker to extract the juice. Discard it.

Return the open cooker to low heat and add the remaining water and the sugar, stirring constantly. When the sugar has dissolved, increase the heat to high and boil the marmalade rapidly for 40 minutes or until setting point is reached.

To test for setting point, remove the cooker from the heat. Put a spoonful of the marmalade on a cold saucer. Cool quickly. If the surface sets and wrinkles when pushed with your finger, the marmalade is ready. If you have a sugar [candy] thermometer, when the temperature reaches 105°C (220°F), the marmalade is ready.

Set the marmalade aside for 10 minutes to prevent the peel from rising to the tops of the jars.

Ladle it into clean, warm, dry jars to within 1.5cm (½in) of the tops. Wipe the rims inside and out to remove any stickiness. Place a waxed paper circle in each jar. When the jars are cool, cover with cellophane fastened with elastic bands. Alternatively, seal with parafin wax. Label the jars and store in a cool, dry place.

PLUM JAM

about 2.25kg (5lb)
5 minutes MEDIUM pressure

Metric/Imperial

1.5kg (3lb) plums, halved and stoned
300ml (10fl oz) water
1.5kg (3lb) sugar

American

3lb plums, halved and pitted
1¼ cups water
6 cups sugar

Remove the trivet. Put the plums in the cooker and pour over the water. Bring to MEDIUM pressure and cook for 5 minutes.

Allow the pressure to reduce at room temperature.

Stir in the sugar in the open cooker over low heat. When the sugar has dissolved, increase the heat to high and boil rapidly for 25 minutes or until setting point is reached.

To test for setting point, remove the cooker from the heat and put a spoonful of the jam on a cold saucer. Cool quickly. If the surface of the jam sets and wrinkles when you push it with your finger, the jam is ready. If you have a sugar [candy] thermometer, when the temperature reaches 105°C (220°F), the jam is ready.

When setting point is reached, skim off the scum from the surface with a metal spoon.

Ladle the jam into warm, dry, clean jars to within 1.5cm (½in) of the top. Wipe inside and outside the rims with a damp cloth to remove any stickiness. Place a waxed paper circle in each jar. When the jars are cool, cover with cellophane fastened with elastic bands. Alternatively, seal with parafin wax. Label the jars and store in a cool, dry place.

LEMON JELLY MARMALADE

about 2.25kg (5lb)
8 minutes MEDIUM pressure

Metric/Imperial

1kg (2lb) lemons
800ml (1¼ pints) water
sugar

American

2lb lemons
3 cups water
sugar

Scrub the lemons. Cut them in half and squeeze out the juice. Remove the pith [white membrane] from the peel and chop the peel finely. Tie the peel in a piece of cheesecloth.

Remove the trivet. Put the water, pips [pits], pith [white membrane], pulp, juice and the cheesecloth bag containing the peel into the cooker. Bring to MEDIUM pressure and cook for 8 minutes.

Allow the pressure to reduce at room temperature.

Remove the cheesecloth bag and transfer the peel shreds to a strainer. Pour boiling water over them and set aside.

Pour the marmalade mixture into a scalded jelly bag or large square of cheesecloth hung over a large bowl. Allow the juice to drain for at least 12 hours. Do not squeeze the bag as this might make the jelly cloudy.

Measure the juice and return it to the rinsed cooker. Add 450g (1lb) [2 cups] of sugar to every 600ml (1 pint) [2½ cups] of liquid. Place the open cooker over low heat and stir until the sugar has dissolved. When the sugar has dissolved, increase the heat to high and boil the marmalade rapidly for about 45 minutes or until just before setting point. Skim the marmalade and add the shredded peel. Continue boiling until setting point is reached.

To test for setting point, remove the cooker from the heat. Put a spoon of marmalade on a cold saucer. Cool quickly. If the surface sets and wrinkles when pushed with your finger, the jelly is ready. If you have a sugar [candy] thermometer, when the temperature reaches 105°C (220°F), the jelly is ready.

Allow the marmalade to stand for 10 minutes to prevent the peel from rising to the tops of the jars.

Ladle the marmalade into warm, clean, dry jars to within 1.5cm (½in) of the top. Wipe inside and outside the rims with a damp cloth to remove any stickiness. Put a circle of waxed paper in each jar. When the jars are cool, cover with cellophane fastened with elastic bands. Alternatively, seal with parafin wax. Label the jars and store in a cool, dry place.

SLOE JELLY

about 3.5kg (8lb)
5 minutes MEDIUM pressure

Metric/Imperial

1kg (2lb) sloes, trimmed and washed
450g (1lb) cooking apples, cut into
    quarters
juice of 1 lemon
sugar

PRESERVES

American

2lb sloes, trimmed and washed
1lb cooking apples, cut into quarters
juice of 1 lemon
sugar

Remove the trivet.

Using a large needle, prick the sloes all over and place them, with the apples, in the cooker. Add enough cold water to cover the fruit and add the lemon juice. Bring to MEDIUM pressure and cook for 5 minutes.

Allow the pressure to reduce at room temperature.

Hang a scalded jelly bag or large square of cheesecloth over a large bowl. Pour the sloe and apple pulp into the cloth. Allow the juice to strain for at least 12 hours. Do not squeeze the bag or the jelly might become cloudy. When the juice has completely drained through, discard the fruit pulp.

Measure the quantity of juice and return it to the rinsed cooker. Add 450g (1lb) [2 cups] of sugar for every 600ml (1 pint) [2½ cups] of juice. Place the open cooker over low heat and stir in the sugar. When the sugar has dissolved, increase the heat to high. Boil the mixture, without stirring, for about 20 minutes or until setting point is reached.

To testing for setting point, remove the cooker from the heat and put a spoon of the jelly on a cold saucer. Cool it quickly. If the surface sets and wrinkles when pushed with your finger, the jelly is ready. If you have a sugar [candy] thermometer, when the temperature reaches 105°C (220°F), the jelly is ready.

Using a metal spoon, skim the scum off the surface of the jelly.

Ladle the jelly into warm, clean, dry jars to within 1.5cm (½in) of the top. Wipe inside and outside of the rims of the jars to remove any stickiness. Put a circle of waxed paper in each jar. When the jars are cool, cover with cellophane fastened with elastic bands. Alternatively, seal with parafin wax. Label the jars and store in a cool, dark, dry place.

Clear, sparkling Sloe Jelly is economical to make as the sloes — the fruit of the common blackthorn tree — can be gathered wild in autumn. Serve with bread and butter or as a condiment with roasts.

BRAMBLE JELLY

about 1.25kg (2½lb)
5 minutes MEDIUM pressure

Metric/Imperial

2kg (4lb) fresh blackberries, hulled
   and washed
300ml (10fl oz) water
sugar

American

4lb fresh blackberries, hulled and
   washed
1¼ cups water
sugar

Remove the trivet. Put the blackberries and water in the cooker. Bring to MEDIUM pressure and cook for 5 minutes.

Allow the pressure to reduce at room temperature.

Hang a scalded jelly bag or square of cheesecloth over a large bowl. Pour the blackberries into the cloth. Allow the juice to drain through for at least 12 hours. Do not squeeze the bag as this might make the jelly cloudy. When the juice has completely drained through, discard the blackberry pulp.

Measure the juice before returning it to the rinsed cooker. Add 450g (1lb) [2 cups] of sugar for every 600ml (1 pint) [2½ cups] of liquid. Stir in the open cooker over low heat to dissolve the sugar. When the sugar is completely dissolved, increase the heat to high and bring the mixture to the boil. Boil briskly, without stirring, for 20 minutes or until the jelly has reached setting point. Remove the pan from the heat. Test it by spooning a little of the jelly on to a cold saucer. Cool it quickly. If the surface is set and wrinkles when pushed with your finger, the jelly is ready. If you have a sugar [candy] thermometer, when the temperature reaches 105°C (220°F), the jelly is ready.

Skim the foam off the surface of the jelly. Ladle the jelly into warm, dry, clean jars to within 1.5cm (½in) of the top. Put a waxed paper circle in each jar. Wipe inside and outside the rims with a damp cloth to remove any stickiness. When the jars are cool, cover with cellophane fastened with elastic bands. Alternatively, seal with parafin wax. Label the jars and store in a cool, dry place.

FIVE-FRUIT MARMALADE

about 2.25kg (5lb)
10 minutes HIGH pressure

Metric/Imperial

1 orange
1 grapefruit
1 lemon
1.5 litres (2½ pints) water
1 large, tart cooking apple
1 pear
1.5kg (3lb) sugar

American

1 orange
1 grapefruit
1 lemon
6 cups water
1 large, tart cooking apple
1 pear
3lb (6 cups) sugar

With a sharp knife cut the orange, grapefruit and lemon in half. Squeeze the juice and reserve the pips [pits]. Cut up the fruit, with the peel, coarsely. Tie the pips [pits] in a piece of cheesecloth.

Remove the trivet and put the juice, fruit and pips into the cooker. Add half the water.

Peel and dice the apple and the pear. Add them to the cooker.

Bring to HIGH pressure and cook for 10 minutes.

Allow the temperature to reduce at room temperature.

Remove the cheesecloth bag, squeezing it against the side of the cooker with a wooden spoon to extract all the juice. Discard it.

Return the cooker to low heat and add the remaining water and the sugar, stirring constantly. When the sugar has dissolved, increase the heat to high. Boil rapidly for 45 minutes or until setting point is reached.

To test for setting point, remove the cooker from the heat. Put a spoon of marmalade on a cold saucer. Cool quickly. Setting point is reached when the surface sets and wrinkles when pushed with your finger. If you have a sugar [candy] thermometer, when the temperature is 105°C (220°F), the marmalade is ready.

Let the marmalade stand for 10 minutes.

Ladle it into clean, warm, dry jars to within 1.5cm (½in) of the tops. Wipe the inside and outside of the rims with a damp cloth to remove any stickiness. Put a small circle of waxed paper in each jar. When the jars are cool, cover with cellophane, fastened with elastic bands. Alternatively, seal with parafin wax. Label the jars and store in a dry, cool place.

DRIED APRICOT JAM with ALMONDS

about 2.25kg (5lb)
10 minutes MEDIUM pressure

Metric/Imperial

500g (1lb) dried apricots
2 litres (3 pints) boiling water
juice of one lemon
1.5kg (3lb) sugar
50g (2oz) almonds, blanched

American

1lb dried apricots
7½ cups boiling water
juice of 1 lemon
3lb (6 cups) sugar
⅓ cup almonds, blanched

Remove the trivet.

Wash the apricots and put them into the cooker. Pour over the boiling water and leave the apricots to soak for 10 minutes.

Bring to MEDIUM pressure and cook for 10 minutes.

Allow the pressure to reduce at room temperature.

Place the open cooker over low heat and stir in the sugar and lemon juice. When the sugar has dissolved add the almonds and increase the heat to high. Boil the jam rapidly for 30 minutes or until setting point is reached.

To test for setting point, remove the cooker from the heat and put a spoonful of the jam on a cold saucer. Cool quickly. Setting point is reached when the surface of the jam is set and wrinkles when you push it with your finger. If you have a sugar [candy] thermometer, when the temperature reaches 105 °C (220 °F), the jam is ready.

Skim off the foam from the surface of the jam. Allow the jam to stand for 10 minutes. Ladle the jam into warm, dry, clean jars, filling them to within 1.5cm (½in) of the top. Wipe the outside and inside of the rim with a damp cloth to remove any stickiness.

Put a small circle of waxed paper in each jar. When the jars are cool, cover them with cellophane fastened with elastic bands. Alternatively, seal with parafin wax. Label the jars and store in a cool, dry place.

GINGER AND APPLE JAM

about 4kg (8lb)
5 minutes MEDIUM pressure

Metric/Imperial

1 litre (2 pints) water
275kg (6lb) cooking apples
8cm (3in) piece fresh root ginger, peeled and bruised
grated rinds and juice of 4 lemons
2.25kg (4½lb) sugar
350g (12oz) preserved ginger, drained and cut into pieces

American

5 cups water
6lb cooking apples
3in piece fresh root ginger, peeled and crushed
grated rinds and juice of 4 lemons
4½lb sugar
12oz preserved ginger, drained and cut into pieces

Remove the trivet. Pour the water into the cooker.

Peel, core and cut the apples into thick slices. Put the apple slices in the water and tie the apple cores with the root ginger in a piece of cheesecloth. Put the cheesecloth bag into the cooker. Add the rind and juice of the lemons. Bring to MEDIUM pressure and cook for 5 minutes.

Allow the pressure to reduce at room temperature.

Lift out the cheesecloth bag and press it against the side of the pan with a wooden spoon, to extract the juice. Discard the bag.

Add the sugar and the preserved ginger to the open cooker, and stir, over low heat, until the sugar has dissolved. Increase the heat to high and boil the jam rapidly until setting point is reached. This will take approximately 1 hour.

To test the jam for setting, remove the cooker from the heat. Put a spoonful of the jam on a cold saucer and cool it quickly. Setting point is reached when the surface of the jam sets and wrinkles when pushed with your finger. If setting point has not been reached, return the cooker to the heat and continue boiling, testing every few minutes. If you have a sugar [candy] thermometer, when the temperature reaches 105 °C (220 °F), the jam is ready.

When the setting point is reached, skim the scum off the surface of the jam with a metal spoon.

A simple country jam, Ginger and Apple Jam is an interesting mixture of lemon, fresh and preserved ginger and apples. Serve with bread and butter or toast.

Ladle the jam into clean, warm, dry jars to within 1.5cm (½in) of the tops. Wipe the outside and inside rims of the jars with a warm, damp cloth to remove any stickiness.

Put a circle of waxed paper in each jar. When the jars are cool, cover with cellophane fastened with an elastic band. Alternatively, seal with parafin wax. Label the jars and store in a cool dry place.

Making chutney is much easier and quicker if you use a pressure cooker, which also ensures that none of the flavourings are lost during the cooking.

600ml (1 pint) white vinegar
1 teaspoon hot chilli powder
5cm (2in) piece fresh root ginger, peeled and finely chopped
1 garlic clove, crushed
1 teaspoon salt
½ teaspoon grated nutmeg
12 cloves
juice and grated rind of 2 oranges
500g (1lb) soft brown sugar

American

3lb pears, peeled, cored and chopped
2 tart apples, peeled, cored and chopped
2 medium-sized onions, peeled and sliced
1lb raisins
2½ cups white vinegar
1 teaspoon hot chili powder
2in piece fresh root ginger, peeled and finely chopped
1 garlic clove, crushed
1 teaspoon salt
½ teaspoon grated nutmeg
12 cloves
juice and grated rind of 2 oranges
1lb soft brown sugar

Remove the trivet. Put the pears, apples, onions and raisins in the cooker. Pour over half the vinegar. Bring to HIGH pressure and cook for 10 minutes.

Allow the pressure to reduce at room temperature.

Add the remaining vinegar and the rest of the ingredients. Stir thoroughly to dissolve the sugar. Return the open cooker to high heat and bring the mixture to the boil, stirring occasionally. Reduce the heat to low and simmer the mixture, stirring occasionally, for 2 hours or until the chutney is thick.

Remove the cooker from the heat. Ladle the chutney into warm, dry, clean jars. Wipe the inside and outside of the rims with a damp cloth to remove any stickiness. If you are using jars with vacuum-sealed lids, fit these immediately. Alternatively, place a circle of waxed paper in each jar and screw the caps on tightly. Label the jars and write on the date.

Store in a cool, dark, dry place, for at least 6 weeks before serving.

TOMATO AND APPLE CHUTNEY

about 3kg (6lb)
20 minutes HIGH pressure

Metric/Imperial

1.5kg (3lb) tomatoes, blanched, peeled and sliced
1.5kg (3lb) dessert apples, washed, cored and diced
3 large onions, peeled and finely chopped
350g (12oz) sultanas
350g (12oz) raisins
600ml (1 pint) malt vinegar
1½ teaspoons dry mustard
1½ teaspoons ground ginger
1 tablespoon salt
1 teaspoon ground allspice
700g (1½lb) soft brown sugar

American

3lb tomatoes, blanched, peeled and sliced

3lb dessert apples, washed cored and
  diced
3 large onions, peeled and finely
  chopped
2 cups golden raisins
2 cups raisins
2½ cups malt vinegar
1½ teaspoons dry mustard
1½ teaspoons ground ginger
1 tablespoon salt
1 teaspoon ground allspice
1½lb soft brown sugar

Remove the trivet. Put the tomatoes,
apples, onions, sultanas [golden raisins]
and raisins in the cooker. Pour over half
the vinegar. Bring to HIGH pressure
and cook for 20 minutes.

Reduce the pressure with cold water.

Add the remaining vinegar and the
rest of the ingredients. Stir thoroughly
to dissolve the sugar. Return the cooker
to high heat and bring the mixture
to the boil. Reduce the heat to low
and simmer, stirring occasionally, for 2
hours or until the mixture is thick.

Remove the cooker from the heat.
Ladle the chutney into warm, dry, clean
jars. Wipe the inside and outside rims
with a damp cloth to remove any stickiness. If you are using jars with vacuum-
sealed lids, fit these immediately.
Alternatively, place a circle of waxed
paper in each jar and screw the caps on
tightly. Label the jars and write on
the date.

Store in a cool, dry place for at least 6
weeks before serving.

NORFOLK FRUIT CHUTNEY

about 2kg (4lb)
20 minutes HIGH pressure

Metric/Imperial

500g (1lb) apricots, stoned and
  chopped
500g (1lb) tart cooking apples, peeled,
  cored and chopped
2 medium-sized peaches, peeled,
  halved, stoned and chopped
1 medium-sized onion, finely chopped
125g (4oz) raisins
3cm (1in) piece fresh root ginger,
  peeled and finely diced
¼ teaspoon grated nutmeg
½ teaspoon allspice
½ teaspoon dried mustard
finely grated rind of 1 medium-sized
lemon
juice and finely grated rind
of 1 orange
400ml (15fl oz) white wine vinegar
225g (8oz) sugar
225g (8oz) soft brown sugar

American

1lb apricots, pitted and chopped
1lb tart cooking apples, peeled, cored
  and chopped
2 medium-sized peaches, peeled,
  halved, pitted and chopped
1 medium-sized onion, finely chopped
¾ cup raisins
1in piece fresh root ginger, peeled
  and finely diced
¼ teaspoon grated nutmeg
½ teaspoon allspice
½ teaspoon dried mustard
finely grated rind of 1 medium-sized
  lemon
juice of finely grated rind of 1 orange
4 cups white wine vinegar
1 cup sugar
1 cup soft brown sugar

Remove the trivet. Put the apricots,
apples, peaches, onion, raisins, ginger,
nutmeg, allspice, mustard, lemon rind,

*Norfolk Fruit Chutney includes apricots,
peaches, apples, onions, raisins, ginger,
nutmeg and lots of other spices. Serve it
with cheese, bread and beer for a
'ploughman's lunch'.*

orange juice and rind and the vinegar
into the cooker. Bring to HIGH
pressure and cook for 20 minutes.

Allow the pressure to reduce at room
temperature.

Return the cooker to low heat and
add the sugars. Stir thoroughly to
dissolve the sugar. Increase the heat to
high and bring the mixture to the boil,
stirring occasionally. Reduce the heat
to low and simmer the mixture, stirring
occasionally, for 40 to 50 minutes or
until the chutney is very thick.

Remove the cooker from the heat.
Ladle the chutney into warm, dry,
clean jars. Wipe the inside and outside
of the rims with a damp cloth to remove
any stickiness. If you are usnig jars
with vacuum-sealed lids, fit these
immediately. Alternatively, place a
circle of waxed paper in each jar and
screw the caps on tightly. Label the
jars and write on the date.

Store in a cool, dark, dry place for
at least 6 weeks.

BOTTLING

Fruit bottling seems to be rather a dying art in this age of pre-packaged, frozen and canned foods.

However, if fruit is cheap or you grow your own, it is well worth doing and pressure cooking makes it a very simple process.

Fruit must be brought to a high enough temperature to kill off the moulds and yeasts that would cause it to decay. A pressure cooker can sterilize fruit in a matter of minutes and thus provide you with delicious fruit pies and crumbles out of season.

Fruit can be very easily overcooked so LOW pressure is used. Two kinds of jars are available for fruit bottling. One type has a screw-top with a specially surfaced metal cover, a plastic ring and a screw band. After the cover has been fitted the screw band is tightened and then turned back a quarter turn to allow for expansion during processing. When the process is complete the screw band is tightened.

The other type has a clip fastening. A rubber ring is placed on the neck of the jar before the metal or glass cover is fitted. The clips secure this but allow it to lift slightly during processing and then hold it firmly when it vacuum-seals during cooling.

The jars should be checked thoroughly before use. Chipped or cracked jars should be discarded as they are unhygienic and will not seal properly. Check that the rubber rings have not perished. Check also that the screw bands have not rusted.

Fruit for bottling should be ripe and firm, except gooseberries which should be green and hard. There is no point in bottling damaged fruit.

The fruit in each jar should be about the same size and degree of ripeness to ensure it is not overcooked. When preparing fruit such as apples, which discolour when exposed to air, make a solution of 1 teaspoon of salt in 600ml (1 pint) [2½ cups] water to keep the prepared fruit in until it is all ready for bottling. Rinse in cold water just before you pack it

Fruit can be bottled [canned] in clip jars (above) or those with screw tops (below). Pack the fruit first (below left), then pour over the syrup (below centre). After processing, test the seal (below right) by removing the screw ring and lifting the jar by the top. A vacuum should have been formed.

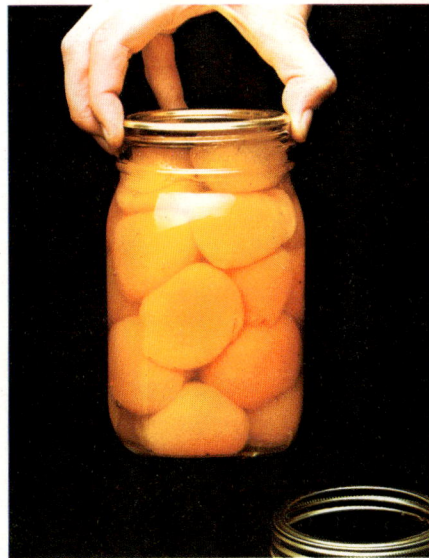

BOTTLING

in the jars. Some hard fruits, such as pears, may not be softened sufficiently during the process as the time taken is very short. They should be put in the cooker and brought to HIGH pressure. Reduce the pressure immediately with cold water and then pack the fruit into jars.

Soak soft fruits in a heavy syrup overnight before bottling. Tomatoes and similar fruits should be peeled by putting them in boiling water for half a minute.

Fruit can be bottled in water but the resulting flavour and colour is generally unsatisfactory. Use granulated sugar and dissolve it in the water according to the following proportions. Boil the solution for 1 minute before use.

A light syrup is suitable for pie fruit. Use 125-150g (4-5oz) [1½-⅔ cup] sugar in each 600ml (1 pint) [2½ cups] water.

A heavier syrup is better suited to dessert fruit. Use 225-275g (8-10oz) [1-1¼ cups] sugar in each 600ml (1 pint) [2½ cups] water.

Wash and rinse the jars thoroughly. Stand them in boiling water.

Clean and prepare the fruit thoroughly. Pack the jars working around the edges. Put each piece of hard fruit in separately.

Make the packing as firm as possible and put in as much fruit as possible without squashing it.

Gradually pour in the boiling syrup, a little at a time. Tap the jars on a work surface or twist them sharply from side to side to release any air bubbles. Leave a ½cm (¼in) space at the top of the jar because the fruit will produce some liquid during processing.

Wipe the tops of the jars with a warm, damp cloth to remove any stickiness. Put on the covers. Screw metal screw-tops tight and then undo a quarter of a turn. Return the jars to the hot water.

Place the trivet upside down in the cooker to prevent the jars standing directly over the heat.

Pour 1 litre (1¾ pints) [1 quart] boiling water into the cooker. Put the jars in the cooker. They will not crack because they have been standing in hot water. Do not let the jars touch each other or the sides of the cooker. Bring to LOW pressure and

A selection of bottled [canned] fruits.
Left to right : Blackberries, cherries, apples, peaches, pears, strawberries, blackcurrants, gooseberries, apricots.

cook for the required time (see chart below).

Allow the pressure to reduce at room temperature. Lift the jars out of the cooker. Tighten the bands of screw-top jars. Set aside.

Next day, check that the jars have sealed. Remove the clips or bands to see if the covers can be lifted. If a vacuum has formed the covers will be firm and the jars can be stored.

If the covers lift, a vacuum has not formed and the jars cannot be stored. Use the fruit immediately and check the equipment before using it again.

To store, wipe the jars clean and wash and dry the clips and bands. Smear a little oil on the covers and bands to prevent rusting. Label the jars (including the date) and store in a cool dark place.

Times for fruit bottling (LOW pressure)

Apples	1 minute	**Peaches**, halved	3 minutes
Apricots	1 minute	sliced	1 minute
Blackberries	1 minute	**Pears**	3 minutes
Blackcurrants	1 minute	**Pineapple**	3 minutes
Cherries	1 minute	**Plums**	1 minute
Damsons	1 minute	**Raspberries**	1 minute
Greengages	1 minute	**Redcurrants**	1 minute
Gooseberries	1 minute	**Rhubarb**, forced	1 minute
Loganberries	3 minutes	garden	2 minutes
Mulberries	3 minutes	**Strawberries**	3 minutes
		Tomatoes (in brine)	3 minutes

BOTTLING

Vegetable bottling needs rather more care than fruit bottling and is not so common. However, with inflation it is worth the time and effort if you grow your own vegetables, or if they are very cheap.

Use the same kinds of jars used for fruit bottling. Wash the vegetables thoroughly in lots of cold water. Scrub root vegetables before peeling. Blanch the vegetables by plunging them into boiling water for the time given in the chart below. Vegetables are bottled in boiling brine made by dissolving 1 tablespoon of kitchen salt in each 600ml (1 pint) [2½ cups] water. Table salt is not suitable.

Unlike fruit, vegetables are not packed tightly. The jars should be well filled but not tightly packed.

Continue as for fruit bottling except use MEDIUM pressure. Green colouring can be added to vegetables which lose their colour, such as peas and beans.

Bottled vegetables are particularly suitable for using in winter stews and casseroles. They are less suited to serving as accompanying vegetables, although they can be quite tasty with the addition of an appropriate sauce.

Times for vegetable bottling (MEDIUM pressure)

	Blanching time	MEDIUM pressure
Asparagus	3	35
Beans, Broad [Lima]	4	40
French [Green]	3	40
Runner	3	40
Beetroot [Beet]	15	40
Carrots	5	40
Celery	6	35
Peas	2	45
Potatoes	5	45
Sweetcorn	3	50

Below: Bottled [canned] fruit can be used for cooking, and will ensure a supply of interesting fruits throughout the year.
Here, bottled [canned] gooseberries have been used for Gooseberry Crumble, served with fresh cream.